CATASTROPHES

Walter R. Brown, Billye W. Cutchen and Norman D. Anderson

Addison-Wesley

ACKNOWLEDGEMENTS

Photographs reproduced through the courtesy of the following:

pages 7, 9, 11, 12, 139, 153	Naval Photographic Center
page 13 (top)	U.S. Information Agency
(bottom)	The Mariners Museum
pages 16, 51, 55	New York Public Library
page 19	Fairfax County, Virginia, Fire & Rescue Service
pages 21, 26	Chicago Historical Society
pages 23, 35	Oregon Historical Society
page 25	The Chicago Tribune. All Rights Reserved.
pages 29, 30–31, 32	National Fire Protection Agency
page 36	The Houston Post Company
pages 43, 46, 67 (top), 97	The Kansas State Historical Society, Topeka
pages 45, 49	The Bancroft Library
pages 52, 56–57, 64, 77, 93, 101, 188	Wide World Photos
page 59	U.S. Geological Survey, Water Resources Division
page 61	Walter R. Brown
pages 67 (bottom), 68, 69	Italian Cultural Institute, New York
pages 73, 74, 80–81	New York Historical Society, New York City
page 85	July 1891 issue of "Century" (adapted from sketch by A. P. Hill)
page 86	July 1891 issue of "Century" (drawing by Charles Nahl)
page 89	July 1891 issue of "Century"
pages 91, 94	California Historical Society, San Francisco
page 99	Library of Congress
pages 107, 111	U.S. Geological Survey, G. .K. Gilbert
page 108	Early engraving. Source unknown.
pages 112–113	U.S. Geological Survey, W. C. Mendenhall
page 114	U.S. Geological Survey, J. R. Balsley
page 117	U.S. Geological Survey
pages 118–119, 121, 122, 124, 125, 134, 140, 143, 145, 146, 155, 156, 160, 162–163, 186	National Oceanic and Atmospheric Administration
pages 127, 128	Source unknown
page 130	Environmental Science Services Administration
pages 131, 168, 183	United Press International
page 133	U.S. Geological Survey, M. L. Fuller
page 149	"Scientific Monthly", December 1939, provided courtesy of Woburn Public Library, Woburn, Massachusetts
page 150	Drawing by Leonard Preston
page 175	Black Star
page 180	British Columbia Government photograph
page 176	Authenticated News Service
page 187	U.S. Geological Survey, D. Dzurisin

Addison-Wesley Publishing Company, Inc.
Reading, Massachusetts 01867
Printed in the United States of America
ABCDEFGHIJK-WZ-79

Library of Congress Cataloging in Publication Data

Brown, Walter R   1929–
  Catastrophes.

  "The material in this book has originally appeared in the Historical catastrophes series."
  Includes index.
  SUMMARY: Describes some of the world's worst natural and man-made disasters throughout history including volcanic eruptions, earthquakes, and fires.
  1. Fires — Juvenile literature. 2. Earthquakes — Juvenile literature. 3. Storms — Juvenile literature. 4. Volcanoes — Juvenile literature. [1. Disasters]
I. Anderson, Norman, 1928–   joint author.
II. Cutchen, Billye W., 1930–   joint author.
III. Title.
TH9448.B75   904'.7   79-19141
ISBN 0-201-00791-6

CONTENTS

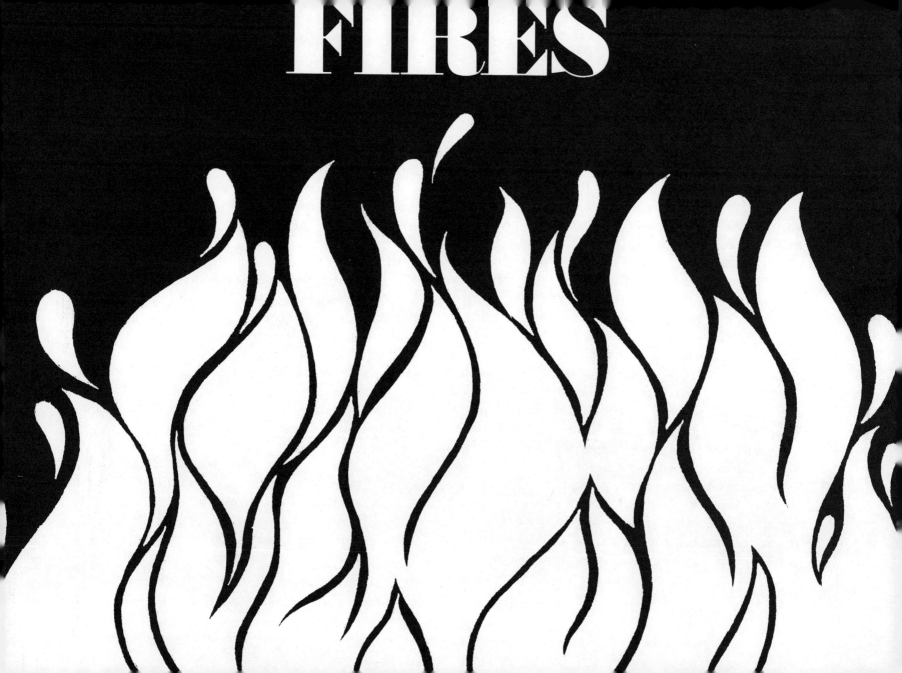

THE END OF THE AGE OF DIRIGIBLES

A LARGE CROWD had waited all day at the Naval Air Station near Lakehurst, New Jersey. Strong headwinds over the Atlantic Ocean had slowed down the world's largest dirigible and she was more than eight hours late in arriving. But at about 4:00 P.M. a man standing on top of a car caught sight of the huge silver airship. He pointed to the northeast and shouted, "There she is!"

The newsreel cameramen hurried to get ready to make movies of the *Hindenburg's* arrival. Present also at Lakehurst were more than a dozen newspaper reporters and photographers. This was her first trip from Germany to the United States during the 1937 season. In spite of the fact that the *Hindenburg* had made ten round trips between Germany and the United States in 1936, her arrival was still a newsworthy event.

American Airlines had a plane waiting to fly passengers departing from the Hindenburg to Newark airport and on to Chicago. One of the reasons for doing this was to promote the DC-3, a new airplane for carrying passengers. There was a lot of argument about whether airplanes or dirigibles were the best way to travel. The airlines were trying to convince people that the DC-3 was a fast, convenient, and safe way to travel.

For the *Hindenburg's* first arrival in 1937, the airlines had flown Herbert Morrison to Lakehurst. He was an announcer for Radio Station WLS in Chicago. With him was his soundman, Charles Nehlsen. From a small wooden shack on the edge of the field, Morrison prepared to describe the landing and then interview some of the arriving passengers. The program was to be recorded and played back Saturday night on the popular radio show, "Dinner Bell."

A landing crew was also waiting around the edge of the field and in a huge hangar building at the Naval Air Station. Besides the 110 Navy men in the landing crew, over 100 additional men had been hired to assist in securing the *Hindenburg* to the tall landing mast. As they went onto the field, a sudden rainstorm sent some of them running for shelter.

Many of the relatives and friends of the passengers aboard the *Hindenburg* waited in automobiles parked near the landing site. When the rain let up they got out of their cars so they would not miss any of the excitement. Among the people who had waited all day were Mrs. Joseph Spah and her three children, Gilbert, Marilyn, and two-year-old Richard. They all were anxious to see their father again. He was an acrobat who was returning from having performed in Europe. He had promised to bring them a dog from Germany and they could hardly wait to see if he had remembered.

Aboard the *Hindenburg,* preparations were being made to land. In the control car, Captain Max Pruss gave orders to the two crewmen who steered the ship. The rudderman, Kurt Schonherr, turned a wheel to steer the ship to the left or right. Eduard Boetius, the elevatorman, moved the controls that made the airship go up or down. This was Captain Pruss's first trip to the United States as commander of the airship. With him in the control car was Captain Lehman, who had commanded the *Hindenburg* on earlier trips. However, he was only along as an observer on this voyage.

Only a little more than 72 hours earlier, on Monday evening, May 3, the *Hindenburg* had gently lifted from the airfield at Friedrichshafen, Germany. As always, her departure was a time of excitement. A German brass band played *Deutschland Uber Alles* ("Germany Over All"). A large crowd waved hats and handkerchiefs and, as the ship got underway, a small group of boys chased after it.

Inside the main compartment, located on the underside of the ship, passengers new to travel by dirigible could not get over the smoothness of the ride. In fact, there was so little feeling of motion that a few of them had cried out in amazement as the ship got underway. As the large cheering crowd was left behind, the hum of the engines could scarcely be heard. The quietness was another advantage of dirigible travel.

Some of the passengers were held in fascination by the breath-taking view from the slanting promenade windows. Many stayed to watch the cities of northern Germany slide by below. A few made a dash to the bar, seeing who could be the first served on this voyage. Others, tired by a day of getting ready for the trip, retired to their staterooms and prepared for a restful night's sleep.

The next morning found the *Hindenburg* over the Atlantic Ocean and headed for New York. By 9:00 A.M. the dining room was filled with passengers hungry for breakfast. Hot rolls, baked in electric ovens, were the pride of Chief Steward Kubis and Chef Maier.

The *Hindenburg* was a symbol of Nazi Germany's boast of world power. Everything possible had been done to make the passengers comfortable in the hope that they would feel kindly about Germany and Adolph Hitler's government. Everything possible also was done to make dirigible travel safe. No one had ever lost his life while traveling on a commercial flight. This was a record that the Germans wanted to keep unbroken.

However, there had been numerous accidents involving military dirigibles. These were a constant reminder of what could happen. Accidents involving U. S. Navy dirigibles had convinced many people there was little future in dirigibles as a means of transportation. The *Shenandoah* had crashed when a violent thunderstorm broke it into three pieces over Ohio in 1925. A violent storm had destroyed the *Akron* off the coast of New Jersey in 1933, killing 73 persons. The *Macon* crashed into the Pacific Ocean in 1935, killing two persons. These accidents ended the construction of dirigibles in the United States.

The *Hindenburg's* designers had done everything possible to make her the safest dirigible ever built. But since she depended on hydrogen for her lifting power, there was always the possibility of a disaster. Thus it was necessary for the crew to take every possible precaution to make certain that a disaster did not occur.

The metal framework of the 803-foot-long *Hindenburg* was covered with a linen fabric. Inside were 16 huge gas bags filled with a total of 7,300,000 cubic feet of hydrogen. Since a mixture of hydrogen and oxygen burns with an explosive force, the bags had to be inspected regularly by the crew for any possible leaks. Also, the dirigible was built so that any leaking gas could escape through the top.

The *Hindenburg* had been designed so that either hydrogen or helium could be used. However, she would have been much safer using helium since this gas does not burn.

The United States was the major producer of helium in the 1930's. Since this lightweight gas was in short supply, the U. S. had passed a law which prevented it from being exported to Germany and other foreign countries. In addition to the shortage, some people were opposed to selling the gas to other countries because they feared that helium-filled dirigibles might be used in warfare.

A series of catwalks and ladders ran through the interior of the *Hindenburg*. These were covered with rubber to prevent a spark which might ignite any leaking hydrogen. Crewmen wore either sneakers or felt boots when they moved about inside the ship. When inspecting the gas bags, they put on asbestos suits free from buttons or metal zippers that could give off even the smallest spark.

The *Hindenburg* was powered by four 16-cylinder, Daimler-Benz diesel engines. Each engine produced 1,100 horsepower, and together they pushed the airship forward at a cruising speed of 84-miles-per-hour in still air. The use of diesel fuel was much safer than gasoline, which had been used in some of the earlier dirigibles.

The luggage of all the passengers had been carefully searched before leaving Friedrichshafen. With war clouds over Europe, there was fear of sabotage. All matches and cigarette lighters had been taken from the passengers and crew. This was done before every departure, since smoking was permitted only in a special smoking room.

The air inside the fireproof smoking room was kept at a higher pressure than the air on the outside. This was to prevent any hydrogen gas from leaking in. To enter the smoking room, passengers had to pass through a special set of double doors.

By Thursday morning land was sighted. By this time all of the passengers had become accustomed to the thrills and comforts of travel by dirigible. Many had made new friends and together they looked from the windows to catch sight of familiar landmarks below. Long gone were any worries they might have had about traveling part way around the world while being held up by some seven million cubic feet of explosive hydrogen gas.

Around noon the *Hindenburg* flew over Boston. Crowds of people out for their lunch hour stood motionless and looked up at the beautiful silver dirigible. Ships in the harbor tooted their whistles. Automobiles stopped and the passengers got out to watch. In the dirigible, the travelers crowded around the windows and pointed to the Custom House tower and other buildings they could recognize.

The *Hindenburg* reached New York City at about 3:00 P.M. First she flew over Times Square where thousands could see her. Traveling southward she passed over the Statue of Liberty and then swung eastward to cross over Ebbet's Field in Brooklyn. The baseball game between the Dodgers and the Pittsburgh Pirates stopped long enough for the fans and players to watch the airship pass overhead. The huge black swastikas on her vertical tail fins gleamed in the bright sunlight.

After flying on past the Empire State Building where photographers on the observation deck

The Shenandoah under construction.
She crashed in a thunderstorm in 1925.

snapped pictures, Captain Pruss pointed his ship toward Lakehurst. When she arrived there around 4:00 P.M., the black clouds of a summer thunderstorm could be seen in the west. As he passed over the airfield, Captain Pruss dropped a message which read, "Riding out the storm."

The *Hindenburg* cruised southward across New Jersey waiting for a radio message from Lakehurst saying it was safe to land. A few minutes after six, a message came in from the Naval Air Station: CONDITIONS NOW CONSIDERED SUITABLE FOR LANDING PERIOD GROUND CREW IS READY PERIOD THUNDERSTORM OVER PERIOD STATION CEILING 2000 FEET PERIOD VISIBILITY FIVE MILES TO WESTWARD PERIOD SURFACE TEMPERATURE 60 PERIOD SURFACE WIND WESTNORTHWEST EIGHT KNOTS GUSTS TO 20 KNOTS PERIOD SURFACE PRESSURE 29.68.

A few minutes later a second message was received which read: RECOMMEND LANDING NOW COMMANDING OFFICER. Captain Pruss radioed back that the *Hindenburg* was on her way back to the landing site. At 7:04 P.M. the *Hindenburg* passed over the airfield at an altitude of about 600 feet and traveling in a northeasterly direction. Captain Pruss ordered the ship to turn to the port, or left, and brought her around in a big circle so that the ship approached the landing mast from the west.

At 7:19 P.M. some of the hydrogen was ordered released and the ship leveled off under perfect control. When her nose was about 700 feet from the landing mast, her four engines were reversed. Forward motion quickly slowed and then stopped. The first landing rope, some 400 feet long and two inches thick, was dropped.

As the *Hindenburg* approached the landing mast, the sun broke through the clouds. On the ground Herbert Morrison had started recording for his radio broadcast.

"Here it comes, ladies and gentlemen, and what a sight it is, a thrilling one, a marvelous sight . . . The sun is striking the windows of the observation deck on the westward side and sparkling like glittering jewels on the background of velvet . . ."

At that moment it was exactly 7:25 P.M. The *Hindenburg's* engines were turning very slowly. The airship was only about seventy-five feet above the ground. Suddenly the people on the ground saw a burst of flame on the top of the ship just ahead of where the upper tail fin joined the hull.

"Oh, oh, oh . . . !" Morrison gasped into his microphone. "It's burst into flames . . . Get out of the way, please, oh my, this is terrible, oh my, get out of the way, please! It is burning, bursting into flames and is falling . . . Oh! It's a terrific sight . . . Oh!"

On the ground one of the landing crew yelled, "Run for your lives!" A member of the landing crew later told what he had done when the command came. "With several of the others I ran as far out of the landing circle as I could. I saw the ship just sink down and the flames go through it. The fabric burned away in just a few seconds. I turned back with the others to go as close to the ship as possible to pick up survivors."

A dairyman, Alfred Snook, was just getting out of his car in the parking lot about 700 feet from the airship. "I saw a burst of flames from the dirigible," he said. "It seemed to come from the rear of the ship. Then there was a terrific explosion and the entire airship was suddenly enveloped in flames. The nose of the airship was jerked upward and then the whole flaming hulk plummeted to the ground where the wreckage was instantly enveloped in a dense black smoke."

As the *Hindenburg* settled toward the ground, some of the passengers jumped from the burning ship. George Willens, a cameraman, was about three-hundred feet away. He reported, "I saw a man hurl himself from the window of the ship, drop about 40 feet to the ground, get up limping, and brush himself off. I was taking a movie of it and yet I could hardly believe my eyes."

Willens ran over and asked the man, "How in the earth did you do it?"

As the great German dirigible Hindenburg drifted slowly in for a landing at Lakewood, New Jersey, a sudden flash of flame swept the tail section.

"I really don't know," replied Joseph Spah, the acrobat whose wife and three children were waiting for him in the crowd. Spah felt himself to see if he was really there. "Whew, am I lucky—not a scratch."

One of the passengers was Mr. George Grant, a distant relative of President U. S. Grant. While waiting for the airship to be secured so they could get off, he and a group of his friends were in the observation salon talking about the crossing.

"Suddenly there was a crumbling sound and an explosion," he said. "The ship dipped sharply and I was thrown forward. There were three windows open and I jumped out of one."

On the ground Mr. Grant couldn't believe that he wasn't hurt. Suddenly a body struck him on the back, smashing him to the earth. It was one of his friends who had jumped out after him.

The escape of Werner Franz, a fourteen-year-old cabin boy, was almost unbelievable. He had been in the officers' dining room when the explosion occurred. He fell as he tried to get to an open hatch, but finally made it. As he jumped, the blazing dirigible settled down around him. Then a water tank above him burst and he was drenched by two tons of water. He scrambled free of the burning wreckage and escaped, wringing wet but with only minor burns.

Members of the landing crew and others on the ground helped get the survivors out and away from the burning ship. Gill Wilson, New Jersey aviation director, praised the work of the men. "Those boys

Fire at sea is also dangerous. Here the Morro Castle is burning in a 60-mile-an-hour wind.

dived into the flames like dogs after rabbits," he said, "but people in the belly of the ship had absolutely no chance."

Captain Lehman, the former *Hindenburg* commander who was an observer on the trip, was one of those who managed to get out. "I don't understand it," he gasped as he staggered from the burning control car. He was taken to a Lakewood hospital suffering from burns and he died the next afternoon. The final death toll was 36. Of these, 22 were crewmen, 13 were passengers, and one was a member of the ground crew.

Captain Lehman wasn't the only one who was unable to understand what caused the disaster. At the time of the calamity, Count C. G. von Zepplin, a nephew of the German inventor of the dirigible, was in Chicago on a business trip. He expressed the opinion that the explosion might have been caused by sabotage. He pointed out that the blast came in the rear of the ship, whereas the gas bags were located in the middle third.

A commission was appointed by the United States Department of Commerce to investigate the cause of the disaster. They ruled out sabotage, although there are still those that believe that this was the cause. Instead, the commission blamed the disaster on St. Elmo's fire, a form of static electricity. The true cause of the explosion probably never will be known.

The scrap metal from the burnt wreckage was shipped back to Germany. There it was melted down and made into airplanes. This was soon to become the fate of all the remaining German dirigibles.

In 1938 the Germans completed work on a new dirigible, the LZ-130. When the United States continued to refuse to sell helium to Germany, the new airship was filled with hydrogen. After the *Hindenburg* disaster, no one seriously considered using a hydrogen-filled dirigible to carry passengers. Germany's newest giant of the sky was equipped with electronic equipment and flown along the coast of England to study British radar. In 1940 she was ordered destroyed and her aluminum used to make dive-bombers. The Age of Dirigibles had come to an end.

Are the days of the dirigible gone forever? Maybe not. In light of our present environmental problems and energy crisis, one scientist recently suggested that we start building dirigibles again. The dirigible could be a means of "clean" transportation. Its energy needs are low and it should be possible to use nuclear power to propel it. Even if diesel engines were used, it would make far less noise and pollution than today's jet aircraft. The dirigible can land in a small area and thus thousands of acres of land needed for a modern airport could be preserved as parks. Filled with helium and built using engineering ideas like those used in the space program, the new dirigible would be safe and an inexpensive way of transporting heavy cargoes.

Who knows, maybe some day soon we will be able to look skyward and thrill at the sight of a new generation of dirigibles!

THE CHICAGO FIRE OF 1871

THE FALL OF 1871 had given Chief Fire Marshall Robert Williams and the 185 men of the Chicago Fire Department a real workout. During the first week of October there had been 20 bad fires. Any one of them could have resulted in a major disaster if it had gotten out of control.

There were two reasons for the large number of fires. Chicago was a rapidly growing city with many wooden buildings. And the summer and fall of 1871 had been very hot and very, very dry.

Forty-one years before, in 1830, Chicago had been only a small fort and trading post with a total population of 170. Then the population began to boom. By 1840, 4,800 lived in the town. People poured into the area looking for jobs and a way to make their fortunes. And many of them did make fortunes, because Chicago was a beehive of activity. During the next 20 years, Chicago became the center of the nation's railway system. By 1860, the population had reached 110,000.

The Civil War did little to slow Chicago's growth. When the war was over, the building boom increased all the more. In 1865, the year the war ended, over 7,000 new buildings were erected at a cost of seven million dollars.

By 1871, Chicago had a population of 334,000 —over three times as many people as ten years earlier. More people meant more buildings —more houses, more offices, more stores, more factories, more schools, more churches. Some of the new buildings were made of brick or stone, but most of Chicago's 60,000 buildings were made of wood. Even the 561 miles of sidewalks were mostly made of wooden planks.

Chicago's huge expanse of wooden buildings was a kindling box for fire. In 1870 over 700 fires were recorded. But because of the dry weather, 1871 was even a worse year.

On July 3, Chicago had one and one-half inches of rain. As people celebrated the Fourth of July, they hoped that the long dry spell was over. But from July 3 to October 9, a period of almost a hundred days, only two and one-half inches of rain fell. Usually Chicago could expect about nine inches of rainfall during that period of the year.

Because of the dry weather the leaves had fallen off the trees earlier than usual. These dry leaves covered the ground where the grass had long since turned brown because of the drought. Here was more fuel for fire!

To make matters worse, a strong southwesterly wind blew almost constantly during the first week of October. In addition to drying things out even more, the wind promised to spread any fire that did get started.

Tired from fighting more than 20 major fires during the past week, Chicago's firemen were unable to stop the blaze.

About 10:00 P.M. on Saturday, October 7, fire broke out in the boiler room of a woodworking shop on Canal Street. The fire soon spread to the stacks of lumber and the piles of scrap wood. By the time the fire department reached the scene, the shop was gone and the fire was being pushed toward the northeast by the strong wind. Soon four blocks of buildings, including several lumber yards, were ablaze.

Chicago's firemen had been fighting fires all week and they were exhausted when they arrived at this new blaze. The 185 firemen had only 17 horse-drawn engines to protect the 36 square miles of city. Chief Williams had begged and pleaded with the City Council for more men and equipment. He also had asked for a fireboat to protect the 13 miles of river front. These waterways were lined with wooden docks and warehouses, and were spanned by 24 wooden bridges.

Chief Williams also was aware of the dangers in the downtown area. Even though the new buildings were of brick and stone, they often had upper stories made of wood and their roofs were usually covered with tar. Many buildings were separated from each other by walls of wooden lath and plaster. Canvas awnings and wooden signs on the store fronts provided natural bridges for fire to travel from building to building.

Chief Williams' job was to do the best he could with the men and equipment that he had. When he saw the size of the fire on the night of October 7, he called out all of his equipment and men. He also enlisted the help of hundreds of spectators in battling the blaze. Homeowners and businessmen whose property was in the path of the fire gladly joined the fight to save their homes and stores.

Dan Quick's saloon was one of the buildings in the direct path of the oncoming flames. Some of the men in the Saturday night crowd had already done more than their share of weekend celebrating. But when Dan Quick promised them all they could drink, they pitched in to help wet down the walls and roof. The saloon was saved.

The firemen and volunteers fought the blaze for over 12 hours before it was finally brought under control. More than four square blocks of the city had been destroyed and buildings valued at over $750,000 lay in ruins.

At three o'clock Sunday afternoon the first firemen were able to return to their stations. Of Chicago's 185 firemen, 60 went home suffering from burns, exhaustion, and smoke inhalation.

Two valuable pieces of fire-fighting equipment, the William James Engine No. 3 and Liberty Engine No. 7, had been damaged and both were sent to the repair shop. The Chicago Engine No. 5 was damaged but still usable. One of Chicago's four hook-and-ladder wagons had been destroyed in the fire.

Patrick and Catherine O'Leary and their five children lived at 137 De Koven Street, about eight blocks south of Canal Street, where the Saturday night fire had started. The O'Leary's were not threatened by the fire since the wind pushed the flames to the northeast and away from where they lived.

The O'Leary family lived in a small wooden cottage on the back part of their narrow lot. In the front was another house which they rented to a family by the name of McLaughlin. To the rear of the O'Leary cottage stood a barn, where five cows, a calf, and a horse were kept. The top part of the barn was filled with two tons of hay, which was used to feed the animals.

Somewhere between 8:30 and 9:00 Sunday evening, October 8, Mrs. O'Leary lit a kerosene lamp and went out to the barn. Why she was there several hours after the cows were usually milked is not known for certain. Some said she was in the barn to check on a sick cow. Others said she was getting some fresh milk for the McLaughlin's, who were giving a party for a relative who had just arrived from Ireland.

Mrs. O'Leary set the lamp on the barn floor. No sooner had she done so than one of the cows kicked it over. The kerosene spilled on the wooden boards of the barn floor and they immediately caught on fire. The flames quickly spread to some dry hay piled nearby.

"Help! Come quick! The barn's on fire!" shouted Mrs. O'Leary.

Her husband, Patrick, rushed out of the house to see what the shouting was about. Mrs. O'Leary's call for help also aroused neighbors and some came running with buckets of water. By now the whole barn was ablaze and the animals trapped inside could be heard trying to escape.

"Peg Leg" Sullivan, who lived just down the street, charged into the barn and grabbed the frightened calf. As he pulled the calf toward the door, his peg leg slipped into a crack between the boards of the wooden floor. Heat from the fire became almost unbearable as he reached down to unfasten the straps on his leg. Then, leaning on the calf, he managed to hop to safety on his one good leg. The calf was the only animal that was saved from the barn.

Another neighbor ran three and one-half blocks to the nearest alarm box, located at Burno Goll's Drug Store. The new pull-type alarm boxes had been installed just a month before. The boxes were kept locked to prevent children from turning in false alarms. The key was left with someone who lived near the alarm box. In this case, the key was kept in the drug store.

When Burno Goll finally found the key, unlocked the box, and pulled the alarm, nothing happened. The Fire Department had failed to test the connections on the recently installed alarm box and it didn't work.

As the fire became hotter, the hay in the loft of the O'Leary's barn exploded, blowing off the roof with a loud roar. Blazing pieces of wood and hay were carried by a 30 mile-an-hour wind to nearby buildings. Soon another barn, a paint shop, and the cottage next door were all burning.

The fire watchman in the tower of the Courthouse near the center of the city saw the glow of the fire in the night sky. He estimated the location of the fire and shouted, "Fire at Canalport and Halstead!" The night telegraph operator pulled the signal for Box 342. Unfortunately, the watchman had guessed wrong about the location of the fire. As a result, all but one of Chicago's fire companies went rushing to a site more than a mile south and west of the fire on De Koven Street.

The Little Giant Engine Company No. 6 was located only five blocks south of the fire. Its night watchman had awakened the men when he saw the roof blow off of the O'Leary barn. The alarm came just a few minutes after the men had gone to bed. They were exhausted from having fought the Saturday fire throughout the night and through much of Sunday. They groaned and complained as they quickly harnessed the horses. One fireman wished aloud, "I sure hope this is a little one so I can get back to bed."

The Steamer was on its way in a matter of minutes. The firebox under the boiler had been filled with fuel before the firemen had gone to bed. As the Steamer lurched into motion, one of the firemen ignited the fuel. The fuel heated the water in the boiler and made the steam that was to operate the pump.

The four horses pulling Engine No. 6 made it to 137 De Koven Street in record-breaking time. The pressure was up in the boiler and the engine was ready to pump when they arrived. William Musham, the engine company foreman, ordered his men to run a hose into the alley behind the burning barn. He hoped that he would be able to hold the fire in a small area. However, the rising wind sent burning materials streaming toward the northeast.

As the fire grew, the watchman in the Courthouse tower realized he had been wrong about the location of the fire. This time he estimated that the fire was at 12th and Johnson, which was only about seven blocks from its true location. When the watchman called out his correction, the telegraph operator refused to send it.

"It will only confuse the drivers," he said. "Besides, they will be sure to see the fire on their way to Canalport and Halstead."

These mistaken directions about the location of the blaze destroyed almost any chance the men had of putting the fire out. When Chicago Engine No. 5 finally reached the O'Leary house, its hose burst and its pump broke down. By the time repairs had been made, the engine had used up its supply of coal in the boiler. Meanwhile the Fire Department telegraph system continued to signal 3-4-2 and the

Even today fire can consume a house in very little time.

remaining companies were busy looking for a fire a mile away.

About 10 P.M. some flaming material hit the steeple of St. Paul's Catholic Church, six blocks north of the O'Leary property. In moments the entire structure was ablaze. The burning church, in turn, set off fires in the huge Bateham Shingle Mill and two furniture factories close by. Altogether these buildings contained 500,000 board feet of lumber and 1000 cords of wood. It was just a matter of minutes before 30 acres of buildings were burning.

At about 11:30 P.M. some burning planks were hurled by the force of the fire across the South Branch of the Chicago River. This was the last natural barrier before the fire reached Lake Michigan on the east and Lincoln Park on the north. Now the fire raced forward through the downtown area of Chicago. Little, short of a miracle, could stop it.

Around midnight the Chicago Gas Light Works caught on fire. People ran like frightened animals, expecting an explosion at any moment. The gas, however, had been pumped into tanks on the north side of town and the expected gas explosion never came. Instead, the burning gas works set the armory on fire and the exploding ammunition was all the more reason to flee from the area.

By now Mayor Roswell B. Mason had telegraphed other cities requesting that firemen and equipment be sent. Trains were soon loaded in cities as far away as New York. The fire department of Aurora, Illinois, thirty-six miles away, was the first to have equipment on the scene.

Meanwhile the fire continued to consume block after block of the business district. At about 1:30 A.M. a burning plank sailed through the air like a spear and crashed into the Courthouse tower. The men already battling small roof fires on the Courthouse did their best to put out this new fire in the tower. But within a few moments the entire tower was ablaze. There was barely time to release the 350 prisoners jailed in the Courthouse before the roof caved in.

Once released, the prisoners looted a nearby jewelry store. But they weren't the only ones who tried to get rich by stealing from the stores and offices in the path of the fire. Chicago's 425 policemen couldn't be everywhere at once. Even after soldiers were brought in to help the police, there was widespread looting.

As the fire raced northward, many people in its path didn't know of the danger. Samuel Stone, assistant librarian of the Chicago Historical Society, was awakened from his sleep by the loud ringing of his house bell. Someone at the door was yelling, "The city is on fire!"

Quickly dressing, Stone left the house. It was almost exactly 2:00 A.M. as he went out the door. He walked south from his house on North Clark Street and toward the fire. He had no difficulty in finding his way as the entire city was lighted by the fire.

The streets were full of people fleeing from the fire. Many were carrying their most treasured be-

Chicago in flames.

longings. Others carried babies or assisted older people who were having difficulty making their way through the crowds. A few had found wagons whose drivers they hired to transport their property. The drivers often demanded $25 to $100 cash in advance to haul one load to safety. Some hauled the load for a block or two and then demanded more money. Otherwise, they said, they would dump their load into the street.

As Stone got nearer the fire, it became more and more difficult to get through the streets. People were everywhere. He kept glancing upward as he walked, because many people were throwing their property from the upper windows, often only to have some of it break into a thousand pieces on the sidewalks below. A few people grabbed at Stone's clothing, asking him if he had seen a relative or friend from whom they had been separated in the confusion.

When he reached the Chicago River, Stone saw that the Clark Street Bridge was on fire. Across the river and eastward toward Lake Michigan everything in sight was enveloped in flames. Having seen for himself how serious the situation was, Stone then turned back and walked quickly a few blocks north and a block east to the Historical Society Building.

The building housing the Historical Society was believed to be as fire resistant as any building in the city. When Stone arrived, he found great confusion. Dozens of people were trying to get inside to leave boxes and bundles containing valuables.

Surely their things would be safe in the basement of Chicago's safest building, they thought.

Stone told the Librarian-In-Charge of the danger from the approaching fire. He then stationed himself at the basement door and tried to keep people out. Many yelled insults and a few threatened to break down the door. At one point Stone had to open the door to let a janitor come in to fill two pails with water because the wooden sidewalk outside the building had caught on fire.

Soon the people outside stopped yelling and someone called for Stone to come out. Stone pushed a heavy trunk against the door he had been holding. He then climbed up on a stack of newspapers so he could see out a basement window. Every part of the yard outside and the sky above was full of flying sparks. Stone also saw a few firebrands strike the yard. These were blazing boards and planks, propelled through the air by high winds much as leaves are blown about by a breeze.

After the fire many people were to report the high wind that hurled burning planks and pieces of wood for hundreds of feet through the air. Walls of flames swept through whole blocks almost instantaneously. Yet, in parts of the city not touched by the fire, the wind never reached much more than 30 miles per hour.

The gale-like winds were convection whorls, or "fire-devils" as they sometimes are called. These whirling masses of fire and super-heated air are caused by the heat of the fire itself. They can carry burning brands, sparks, and masses of flames forward for distances up to half a mile. New fires may be started by these "fire-devils" far in advance of the fires which created them.

Inside the Historical Society Building, Stone now realized that he had to act quickly. He hurried up one flight of stairs to the reception room and then up another flight to the upper library room. The entire framework of the windows on the front of the building were now burning, with tiny flames hanging like feathers on every inch of the windows.

Stone ran back to the reception room on the first floor. Hanging in a heavy frame on the wall of the reception room was the original copy of Lincoln's Emancipation Proclamation!

President Abraham Lincoln had issued the Emancipation Proclamation on January 1, 1863. The Proclamation freed the slaves in the states which had left the Union at the beginning of the Civil War. The President had donated the original copy to be sold for the benefit of the Chicago Sanitary Fair held in late 1863. The document had been purchased by Thomas B. Bryan who, in turn, had given it to the Soldiers' Home. It had been placed in the Historical Society Building for safe keeping after the new building was completed in 1868.

Stone worked feverishly to get the Proclamation from the frame so he could fold it and place it inside his coat. As he did so the wind filled the air outside with sparks, and firebrands began striking the reception room windows. Sounds from above indicated that the upper windows and roof were beginning to fall.

Combination of strong winds and fire can devastate the wilderness as well as cities.

If he was going to escape from the building, he dared not remain a second longer. Leaving the Proclamation, he ran down the basement stairs two steps at a time. Many of the bundles left in the basement for safe keeping had already caught on fire. Because of the smoke he could hardly find his way to the door. When he pushed the trunk back and looked out, he saw the sidewalk, the front fence, and all of the buildings to the south were ablaze. Firebrands and sparks filled the air, pushed toward the northeast by the wind.

Stone grabbed a shawl from one of the bundles and covered his head and body the best he could. He sprang through the door, raced across the rear yard, and leaped over a low picket fence. Once on Dearborn Street, he dropped the burning shawl and ran northward as fast as his legs could carry him to Erie Street. Part of the way he was followed by a bellowing cow, the hair on her back scorched black by the intense heat of the fire.

Samuel Stone paused on the north side of Erie Street to catch his breath and look back at the burning building from which he had escaped. The entire building was one mass of flames. Even the west side of the building, made of solid brick, was a solid sheet of flame. There was no woodwork on that side to feed the flames, but the wall melted away like butter before his eyes.

Stone thought to himself, "If I had only left the basement and gone upstairs a couple of minutes sooner, I might have saved the Proclamation." For several years after the fire there would be rumors that those freed by the Proclamation would have to return to slavery since the original had been burned. This, of course, was not true.

Stone's thoughts were interrupted by a great blast of wind and smoke. A giant blaze about 200 to 300 feet long and perhaps 150 feet in height passed nearly over him. It was traveling toward the northeast and came down in a shower on the spire of the Church of the Holy Name a couple of blocks away. In an instant the top of the spire was in flames. Soon the church and neighboring buildings were on fire. They burned with such intensity that the smaller ones were reduced to piles of ashes in five minutes or even less. Stone had never seen such a sight.

Stone realized then that he was lucky to have escaped from the Historical Society Building when he did. But he didn't want to trust his luck a second time by remaining on Erie Street too long. Knowing how fast the oncoming fire was traveling, he set off up Dearborn Street on a dead run.

He didn't stop running until he reached the cemetery. Then he slowed to a walk and kept going until he came to Lincoln Park. He joined the thousands who sought safety from the fire there.

Still thousands of others had fled from the downtown area to the lakefront. Some were rescued by boat and taken to points north or south of the part of the city being engulfed by the flames. Others buried themselves in the wet sand and many stood in Lake Michigan with water up to their necks. Additional thousands escaped to the western parts of the city. There they sought shelter with friends and relatives, or slept wherever they could find a place.

At about the same time Stone reached Lincoln Park, the fire had encircled Chicago's new waterworks a few blocks northeast of the Historical Society Building. Located near the lake front, the waterworks was connected by a huge tunnel to an intake station some two miles out in Lake Michigan. As long as the waterworks stood, there was almost unlimited water with which to fight the fire. The waterworks was built in the imitation of an European castle, with stone walls and a slate roof. It was believed to be safe from the fire.

At first the waterworks withstood the heat and flames. Then a blazing timber crashed through the roof and it was only a little while until the whole structure collapsed. Now Chicago had no water except what was in the rivers and in Lake Michigan.

Twice during the night dynamite was used to try to stop the advancing flames. Both attempts failed because the wreckage from the dynamite blasts only speeded up the fire's race from block to block.

All day Monday the fire continued to burn. The few houses and buildings in the downtown district that somehow had been missed by the fire on Sunday night were now set ablaze. Many of these fires were started by the intense heat and sparks from the smoldering piles of debris.

The fire was almost burned out by late Monday afternoon. Fortunately the wind continued to blow toward the northeast. Lake Michigan on the east and Lincoln Park on the north were natural bar-

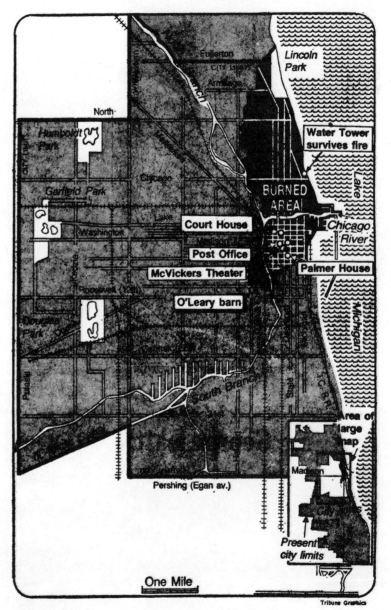

Contemporary map showing the Chicago fire locations.

riers that did as much as anything to check the fire's spread. Shortly before midnight on Monday night, it started to rain and the people of Chicago knew the battle against the fire would soon be over.

On Tuesday morning a new battle began—a battle of finding safe drinking water, food, clothing, and shelter for the 90,000 people left homeless by the fire. Three hundred people had lost their lives. An area of 2124 acres (about three and one-half square miles) in the heart of the city was totally destroyed. The total property loss was estimated at $200,000,000, only part of which was covered by insurance.

Help poured into Chicago by train from cities all over the eastern part of the United States—boxcars full of cooked food, clothing, drinking water, and tools. And the people of Chicago were quick to begin rebuilding their city.

By noon on Tuesday an enterprising real estate salesman had thrown together a wooden shanty in the burned out area and was back in business. The Chicago Board of Trade opened for business, operating around a badly scorched table. Tuesday afternoon the *Tribune* published its Fire Edition on rented presses.

Within a month of the fire 4,000 new buildings had been put up. Two years later the vacant lots in the business district were worth more than the same land, with buildings on it, had been worth before the fire. Chicago was on the move again!

By 1875 few remains of the catastrophe could be seen. Chicago continued to build and to grow—500,000 people by 1880 and over a million residents at the turn of the century. The disastrous fire of 1871 turned out to be only a pause in the history of Chicago's bid to become one of the major cities of the world.

Fireboats hurl streams of water onto burning grain elevators in a recent Chicago fire.

THE WINECOFF HOTEL

No one in the crowd leaving the movie theater noticed the gray-haired man standing on the corner of Peachtree Street and Carnegie Way. They had just sat through the longest movie ever made, the exciting "Gone With the Wind." The story about the Civil War had proven to be a big hit in Atlanta, Georgia, in spite of the shocking use of a swear word by the hero. The elderly man had already seen the show and had decided to walk a few blocks to see Walt Disney's "Song of the South" at another theater.

It was late, but Atlanta's Peachtree Street was ablaze with lights. The man looked down the short block toward Ellis Street. There towered the fifteen story hotel that he had built. He nodded to himself with satisfaction.

"She still looks great!" he thought to himself. "After all these years, she is still a beautiful building."

W. F. Winecoff, the man who stood looking at his creation, had been an excellent builder. When the hotel had opened in 1913, it was the finest construction job in Atlanta and probably in the country. "Completely fireproof," the stories in the newspaper had said. And everyone agreed that there was little in the framework of the building that could burn. The heart of the building was a steel frame. The roof and floors were of concrete. On the outside, the walls were made of brick and were 12 inches thick. And the inside walls were made of tile and plastered on both sides.

Mr. Winecoff had retired from the building business and, after looking around the city, finally decided to live in the hotel that bore his name. He still got a certain thrill when he saw the flashing name WINECOFF in bright neon lights reflecting off the marble front of the hotel. He knew the building well. He had watched every brick and beam being put into it. He felt certain the 33-year-old building was still the safest and best in the city.

It was December 6, 1946. It had been a bad year for hotel fires. Ninety people had died in the month of June alone in fires in hotels in Chicago, Illinois, in Dubuque, Iowa, and Dallas, Texas. But these terrible fires were nothing compared to what was about to happen in Atlanta early the next morning.

The 78-year-old Winecoff hurried down Peachtree Street in the chill midnight air. He entered the large lobby and crossed the heavy carpeted floor to the elevator. He waved to the night clerk behind the registration desk and to the bellman who sat nearby. Somewhere in the building, Winecoff knew, were four other members of the hotel's staff—a building engineer, a night maid, a cleaning woman, and the elevator operator who smiled as the elderly man entered the iron box.

There was no need for her to ask which floor her passenger wanted.

The elevator was in the center of the building. The only stairway in the building led upward alongside it. This wooden stairway branched halfway up, each side leading to one of two long corridors that ran parallel to each other. By this arrangement of corridors it had been possible to get 192 rooms into the box-shaped building.

Mr. Winecoff felt suddenly tired as he left the elevator. As he walked down the long corridor toward his room he hardly noticed the plush carpet under his feet. Either side of the hallway was lined with doors of wood panels set in wooden frames. The hallway and the rooms were wallpapered, and the ceilings were painted. The rooms were full of furniture such as beds, chairs, and dressers. Each window was covered by heavy drapes and some had wooden venetian blinds. Winecoff was a builder, not an interior decorator. He never realized that his "fireproof" building had been filled with almost every type of material that would burn.

Above each door in the hotel was a transom. The building had been built long before the days of air conditioning, and the little opening above the door allowed air to circulate through the rooms. Mr. Winecoff opened his transom wide and then slid one window down a little from the top. Chill, night air flowed through the room as he went to bed.

Several hours later, a little after three o'clock, a buzzer on the switchboard behind the registration desk sounded. The clerk answered the call.

"Room 510," he said to the bellman. "They want some more ice."

"That must be quite a party," the bellman answered with a smile.

"I'll go along with you," the night engineer said. "It's time for me to make my rounds anyway. And maybe you and I will get an invitation to join the party."

And that is exactly what happened. Both men accepted the invitation to have a drink with the guest in 510. As they closed the door, they heard the buzzer sound in the elevator.

On the lobby floor, the young lady who ran the elevator found two of the hotel's guests waiting for her. She took them to the tenth floor and then started down again. As the elevator dropped quickly downward, she suddenly smelled something. When she reached the lobby, she left the elevator and rushed to the registration desk.

"I think something is burning," she told the clerk. "I smelled what must have been smoke, somewhere between the sixth and the third floor."

"Go get the engineer and the bellman! They should be in room 510. Hurry!"

The night clerk left the desk and walked rapidly to the stairway. As he reached the next floor up, which was called the mezzanine, he saw the flickering glow of flames reflecting on the walls from the floor above. He ran quickly to the desk and telephoned the fire department. Then he began the long process of calling each of the 192 rooms to warn the guests.

Meanwhile, on the fifth floor, the elevator operator discovered that the engineer and bellman had already left the party in room 510. As she returned to the elevator, she saw the yellow flames climbing up the open stairwell. In less that a minute, the fire had spread two floors upward!

HOTEL FIRE!

The firemen felt a knot of fear in their stomachs as they rolled from their beds. Dressing quickly and climbing aboard the already-rolling trucks, they each tried to remember the Winecoff Hotel.

"Fifteen stories!" one thought. "The 100-foot ladder will reach the ninth or tenth floor. I hope it started at the top and the people were able to move down, or we will never get to them."

"No fire escape!" another remembered. "Only that one wooden stairway in the middle. And the elevator. If she started in the stairwell, everyone will have to come down the outside."

The Chief, roaring ahead of the string of trucks through the darkened streets, thought back to May 16, 1938. The Terminal Hotel hadn't had an outside fire escape either. He remembered the 38 bodies, most burned beyond recognition, that he had counted as they lay in neat rows in the gutter.

One fire company was only a block away from the hotel and arrived within 30 seconds after the alarm reached them at 3:42. They found flames leaping from the windows of the third, fourth, and fifth floors. As they arrived, a body smashed into the pavement from somewhere in the darkness above the fire.

Even the tallest ladders were unable to reach the people trapped on the top floors of the hotel.

The open staircase was the cause of the rapid spread of the fire. Being made of wood, it provided fuel for the flames. Being open, it acted like a huge chimney and carried both smoke and flames upward. By the time the fire had been discovered, escape by way of the single stairway was impossible.

The elevator was not usable as a way out for the people on the upper floors. Even if the electricity had stayed on, only a fool would have tried to take it up through the blaze and back down again.

The crews of the ladder companies quickly moved into action. The huge ladders were levered into position against the building and firemen scrambled upward as people screamed for help from almost every window. The longest of the ladders reached to the window sills of the tenth floor rooms. The people on the top five floors watched in horror as they realized that the ladders were not able to reach them.

Cut off from the stairway by the flames, some people tried to let themselves down to a lower floor by tying bed sheets together. Many of these makeshift ropes broke or were burned by the flames, dropping dozens of people into the street more than 100 feet below. One man reached for the top of the ladder as it swung toward him, but as he pulled himself out of the window, two bodies falling from the floor above smashed into him and all three people fell to their deaths. A fireman pulled a frightened woman from a window ledge and started down the long ladder when a second woman fell into them from somewhere above. All

Fire in any public place can cause panic. Here are photos taken during and after a circus fire.

three crashed onto the hotel's marquee. The women were killed, the fireman seriously injured.

"Pull three more alarms!" the Chief shouted to his driver. "We can't get into the building at all. We need every piece of equipment in the city!"

More ladders were put against the walls and nets were spread out all around the building. One man died when he missed the net by inches. Others refused to jump and were finally overcome by smoke and flames.

One ladder company carried small ladders to the top of the Mortgage Guarantee Building, which stood across the street from the hotel. Several people escaped by making the shaky passage along the horizontal ladders. One of these was an army major who had spent several years fighting the war in Europe. He later said that the fear he felt while being shot at and bombed was nothing compared to the feelings he had when he realized that they were trapped by the flames.

The transoms over the doors proved to be the instrument of death of many people. Smoke and gases poured through these openings into many rooms, suffocating the people trapped inside. One couple survived by quickly closing the transom and putting the mattresses from the beds against the door. Throughout the fire, they poured water on the mattresses and managed to keep the fire from breaking through.

Within the first few hours, the temperatures in some of the rooms reached 1,500 degrees Fahrenheit. Telephones melted, steel doors twisted, and people died. The super-heated air burned the inside of their lungs with the first breath and, even if they were pulled from the flames, death caught up with them quickly.

It was after nine o'clock the next morning before the fire was out. The room-to-room search for bodies and survivors began. Outside, the hotel was a blackened ruin. Torn and scorched bedsheets hung from the charred windows. Inside almost everything had burned. The carpets were gone. The wooden stairs and most of the doors and door-frames were burned. The drapes and furniture of many of the rooms had been completely burned, leaving the bed and chair springs the only things the firemen could recognize.

Yet the structure itself was still in good shape. The "fireproof" building had stood the test of 1,500 degrees of heat. The deaths were caused by the burning of the furnishings that had been added after the building was completed.

A total of 91 people were seriously injured in the fire. They were taken to the local hospitals and treated.

The smell of burned flesh hung in the air over Atlanta as the Fire Chief made his way down the long row of corpses. There were 119 to count this time. One of these was the charred body of W. F. Winecoff, the builder of Atlanta's greatest hotel.

You might expect that in the many years since 1913, when Winecoff built his hotel in Atlanta, builders and interior decorators would have learned how to make tall buildings really fireproof.

But high-rise buildings still burn and the loss of life in these fires is often quite high.

Early in the morning of February 1, 1974, a secretary turned on six air conditioners on the 12th floor of the new, 26-story Edificio Joelma building in Sao Paulo, Brazil. The heavy motors pulled a surge of electricity through light-weight wires that lay loose on a false fiber ceiling. Within seconds, the wires heated the fiber and the ceiling began to burn.

The secretary saw the smoke almost immediately and tried to fight the fire with an extinguisher. The fire continued to spread, so she called the building's maintenance office. By the time a man from that office arrived, the fire was out of control.

Ten of the floors below the fire were used for parking cars. The 14 floors above were all offices, where more than 600 people were already at work. Many of these people tried to escape down narrow, open stairways. Others rang repeatedly for the elevators.

More than 150 employees headed for the roof. Once out in the open, they found the roof top divided by a concrete water tower. It was necessary for each person to decide whether he would go to the half of the roof on the north or go toward the south. The 60 people who chose the south side of the roof died as the flames from below curled up over the edge of the building. More than 40 people jumped to their deaths as the smoke and flames threatened them. And nearly a hundred more bodies were found in the smoking ruins.

FIRES AND FIRE FIGHTERS

CAN YOU IMAGINE a life without fire? Think of all the ways we use this amazing chemical reaction almost every hour of every day. We heat our homes, cook our food, even move ourselves from place to place using heat from fires. Did you know that almost all of the electricity we use in our homes and schools still comes from generators turned by steam made by burning coal and oil?

But each year in the United States, about 12,000 people lose their lives in fires and another 120,000 people are injured. Two and three-quarters billion dollars worth of property is also burned each year. Considering the number of people in this country, the United States has the poorest record of fire prevention in the world. Americans do not seem to be aware of the danger they face from fires. If they did, perhaps they would insist upon better fire departments and better laws that regulate how buildings are constructed.

A fire starts when a fuel is heated to a certain temperature in an atmosphere that contains oxygen. The heat may come from any of many sources—another fire or a spark, over-heated electric wires, friction, or from the slow combining of something like oil or hay with oxygen.

If enough fuel and oxygen are available, the fire will grow rapidly. Every minute that it burns it can easily double its size. A fire that is just beginning can almost always be put out easily. But if it is allowed to grow, it quickly becomes so large that it is impossible to control.

Since three things are necessary for a fire to burn—fuel, oxygen, and temperature—there are three main ways to control the flames. The fuel can be removed, as you do when you turn off a gas stove. Or the oxygen can be kept from the fuel. Some fire extinguishers produce a gas that smothers the flames. A lid slipped over a pan of burning grease or dirt poured over a camp fire cuts off the supply of oxygen. Cooling the fuel to a temperature below its kindling temperature is the third way. Water puts out fires by cooling the fuel.

Controlling fire so that we can use it in our homes is a fairly simple business. But when a fire gets out of our control, stopping it is often a job for the experts of the fire department.

Let's suppose that you are in a building in which a fire starts. It doesn't make much difference how the fire started—whether it was arson, carelessness, faulty construction, or "an act of God." Once the fire has begun, you must either put it out or get away from it before it kills you.

No building is actually fireproof. Many of the materials used in modern buildings will not burn. The steel, concrete, brick, glass, and metals used today are not fuels. But almost all of the furnishings inside the building will burn. These include not only the carpets, drapes, and furniture, but also the paint and wallpaper on the walls. Many buildings, especially our homes, have many different types of fuels stored in them. These include gasoline and oil in our cars and lawnmowers, fuel for camping stoves and lanterns, paints and painting equipment, old rags, newspapers, and even pieces of wood.

Discovering the fire early, before it reaches the danger level, is important if the blaze is to be controlled. Many large buildings and some homes are now equipped with smoke-and-heat detecting instruments. These gadgets sound an alarm at the first hint of smoke or at any unusual rise in temperature. In buildings that do not have these detectors, alert people must take their places. The smell of smoke must be investigated quickly and thoroughly.

Once the fire is discovered, it must be attacked quickly. Many modern buildings, especially those in which the threat of fire is great, are equipped with sprinkler systems. The heat of the fire causes the sprinkler head, which is usually on the ceiling, to open and spray water onto the fire. In most cases, since the blaze is still small when the sprinkler starts, the fire can be put out by the spraying water. If the fire is too big to be put out by the sprinkler, the water will often keep the fire from spreading very fast. Very few lives are lost in fires that occur in buildings that are equipped with sprinkler systems.

Axes and hoes are still used to fight forest fires, along with modern equipment.

The early use of fire extinguishers can often control or put out a fire. The first job of a person who discovers a fire is to report it so that the fire department can be called. Then, if the fire is still small, a fire extinguisher can be used on it. There are many different types of extinguishers now being sold. Some work well for different types of fires but may not be safe to use in other situations. Everyone should know the advantages and disadvantages of the types of fire extinguishers that he might be called upon to use.

Fire fighters classify fires into four groups. **Class A Fires** are those in which such things as wood or paper are burning. These fires can usually be put out with water. **Class B Fires** are caused by burning liquids, such as gasoline, oil, or alcohol. Putting water on fires of this type usually results in spreading the fire, since the fuel will float on the water. Only carbon dioxide or dry chemical extinguishers can be safely used on these fires. The same type of chemicals can be used on **Class C Fires.** These are caused by electrical wires or equipment that become overheated. If the current is still on, the person trying to put out the fire might be electrocuted if he put water onto the blaze. **Class D Fires** are those rare ones in which certain metals burn. These special chemical fires require specific types of chemicals to put out the fires.

Once a fire is beyond the control of sprinkler systems and small fire extinguishers, it is important that the people in the building get outside as quickly as possible. Fumes and heat from a large

Explosions of different kinds can cause disastrous fires. This is a view of the Monsanto Chemical Company plant which was destroyed by fires caused when a shipload of fertilizer exploded at a Texas City dock.

fire can be picked up by the heating and air conditioning systems of large buildings and carried to places far away from the flames. These fumes and super-heated air can kill people who are safe from the fire itself. Doors should be felt before they are opened and, if they feel hot they should be left closed as a barrier against the flames. People making their way through smoke-filled rooms should stay as close as possible to the floor where the air is less likely to be poisoned by fumes or heated to a dangerous level. Elevators should never be used as escape routes. The electricity used to operate the elevator may be cut off by the fire, leaving the elevator cage stranded between floors and trapping the people inside. Elevator doors that are opened by the breaking of a beam of light may stop on the floor where the fire is the worst and have their doors held open by dense smoke. Everyone who is in a tall building should know exactly where the fire stairs are and how to get to them quickly.

The fire fighters who arrive at a fire have to be in excellent physical condition. Fighting a major fire takes tremendous strength and endurance. The protective clothing that a fire fighter wears into a burning building will weigh more than 20 pounds. To protect himself from the smoke, the fire fighter will usually wear an oxygen tank and mask. These self-contained breathing units may weigh as much as 50 pounds. The weight of the hose and other tools that the fire fighter carries will raise the total weight to more than 100 pounds.

In addition to having to be strong enough to carry his equipment, the fire fighter must be prepared to carry anyone who needs help in getting away from the burning building. He must also be strong enough to hold the hose against the pressure of the rushing water.

And he must be able to work hard in the tremendous heat of a burning building. Fire fighters may be forced to enter a building in which the temperature near the floor is over 500 degrees Fahrenheit. Temperatures near the ceiling, by the way, may reach over 1,500 degrees Fahrenheit —hot enough to melt the glass of the light bulbs!

A generation ago, about all a fire fighter did was to break into a burning building and pour a lot of water onto the flames. Water is still the cheapest and easiest to get of all fire fighting equipment. But things are changing very rapidly. Scientists all over the world are experimenting with different ways to put out fires. Various foams, dry chemicals, and gases are now being tried. The fire fighter of the future will find his job changing very rapidly.

As fire fighting equipment changes, the fire fighter must constantly learn new techniques. It takes intelligence as well as muscle to be a modern fire fighter. Most fire departments require that their new employees have at least a high school diploma, and many departments are requiring some college work in subjects related to fire fighting. In addition, each new fire fighter must spend several weeks in training before he is allowed to go into active service. Once he is on the job, the fire fighter's schooling continues. For several hours each day, each fire fighter in most departments must study and train.

In order to do his job well, the fire fighter must understand some of the basic science principles that are taught in courses in physics, chemistry, and mathematics. He must know what chemical reactions take place when certain materials burn. He must know what will happen if certain chemicals are put on a fire. He must understand how heat travels from place to place and what the effects of heat on different types of building materials will be. And, if he wants to be an officer, he must learn how to handle both people and money efficiently.

Sometime in the future, if present trends continue, fire fighting will be done by teams of people trained in very specialized skills. Some employees of the fire department may specialize in preventing fires through education and the inspection of buildings. Other fire fighters will inspect and install smoke-and-heat detecting equipment, alarm systems, and fire-escape equipment. Almost every fire department in the future will probably hire people who are expert chemists to direct the handling of all types of dangerous materials. And, of course, there will always be a need for these fire fighters who must attack the flames directly, risking their lives to save the lives and property of people.

FLOODS

"THE PALM OF THE HAND OF GOD" (IMPERIAL VALLEY, CALIFORNIA)

THIS IS THE STORY of a very unusual flood. It lasted for two years, caused millions of dollars in damages, left behind a lake that can still be seen more than 70 years later, but killed no one. This is also the story of men who wanted to make the desert bloom, men who wanted to make money quickly and who didn't care about the welfare of anyone else, and about men who learned to control a huge river. But most of all, this is the story of a desert basin in southern California.

The low-lying desert area was called *La Palma De La Mano De Dios*—The Palm of the Hand of God—by the Spanish-speaking people who lived nearby. Its history began many centuries ago. At least, the valley was formed long before anyone began keeping a history of the region that now lies on the border between California and Mexico.

Geologists, scientists who study the earth and its history, tell us that at one time the Gulf of California ran many miles much farther to the north than it now does. Near the northern end of the Gulf, the water must have stood nearly 300 feet deep. Into this large arm of the ocean flowed the river we now call the Colorado.

Rain that falls on parts of Wyoming, Colorado, Utah, New Mexico, Arizona, Nevada, and California finds its way to the sea through the Colorado River. The river also carries along with this water tons of silt and sand from the surface of the more than a quarter of a million square miles of land that it drains. This is the river that dug out the mile-deep Grand Canyon.

Centuries ago, as this rushing water entered the quiet water of the Gulf of California, it slowed and dropped the load of sediment it was carrying. Slowly this sand and silt accumulated until a huge delta was built at the mouth of the river. As more sediment flowed down from the mountains, the delta grew. Finally the delta became so large that it completely blocked the upper end of the Gulf.

To the north of the delta dam now stood a huge inland salt lake, completely cut off from the sea. The Colorado River found new paths to the Gulf across the delta and no water flowed into the new salt lake. Eventually, over hundreds or perhaps thousands of years, the water in the lake evaporated and left the basin exposed to the air.

This basin is over 200 miles long and nearly 50 miles wide, and more than one-fourth of it is below sea level. Its lowest point is 273 feet below the level of the water in the Gulf of California—almost as low as the more famous Death Valley. To the early Spanish explorers, it looked from the surrounding hills like the depression in an open hand. So, they named it "La Palma De La Mano De Dios."

At first, the early American settlers avoided the

basin, which they called the Salton Sink. The men who rushed to California to look for gold in 1849 found it a place to cross quickly on their way to more pleasant surroundings. In the summer, the temperature in the Sink often reached 125 degrees, and in an average year only three inches of rain fell. To the south and east, between the basin and the Colorado River, stretched an area of sand dunes that were all but impossible to cross on foot or horseback. Beyond the San Bernardino Mountains to the north lay the Mojave desert and Death Valley. Westward, across the crinkly San Jacinto and Laguna Mountains, was San Diego and the Pacific Ocean. In the last years of the 19th century, as California's population grew toward a million, no one lived in the Salton Sink. Then, shortly before 1900, two men came to the desert basin, one with a dream, the other with money and technical knowledge.

The first man was Charles Rockwood, a young engineer and surveyor. His idea was to use the water of the Colorado River to irrigate the rich-but-dry soil of the Sink. He realized that the river was higher than most of the bottom of the basin and believed that a canal could be dug that would allow water to flow downhill into the Sink. It was a good idea and he knew it would work, but he needed money and someone who understood irrigation work.

George Chaffey met both of these requirements. He had just completed a huge irrigation project near Los Angeles and was looking for a place to invest the money he had made and a job that needed his talents. For six weeks the two engineers surveyed the basin and the land around it.

Chaffey liked what he saw. The soil of the Sink was fertile, except for those places that had been spoiled by the salt left when the sea water evaporated. The basin was normally free from frost for more than ten months each year and farmers would be able to get two crops each year under the burning summer sun. Rain fell so rarely that it would never interfere with harvests. And the tracks of the Southern Pacific Railroad passed nearby, so trains would be able to rush fresh fruits and vegetables to New Orleans quickly.

The only real problem seemed to be the digging of the canal. It would be impossible, Chaffey knew, to dig a ditch through the sand dunes that lay between the river and the Sink with the equipment then available. He searched carefully through the dunes until he found a dry riverbed that ran across the delta from Mexico nearly to the entrance of the Sink. The riverbed was full of loose silt and sand and this should have warned Chaffey that the Colorado River had overflowed and used the old river as a drainage canal sometime in the past. But the engineer was anxious to see the project move forward, and he overlooked this evidence.

In November, 1900, work was begun on a stretch of canal that would carry water from the Colorado to the dry riverbed in Mexico. The amount of water that could flow into the canal would be controlled by a huge concrete flood gate. After passing the gate, which stood across the river from Yuma, Arizona, the water would flow toward the south alongside the main channel of the river. Several miles inside Mexico, Chaffey's canal would meet the dry riverbed and the water would flow north again. Short, feeder canals were designed to distribute the water to farms scattered throughout the valley.

Advertisements were sent out all over the country telling people that the valley would soon be ready for farming. But Chaffey was too smart to try to get people to move to a place called the Salton Sink. Instead he called the basin by the name we use today—Imperial Valley.

Settlers flocked into the desert basin with the beautiful name. The first of them found only a wasteland. Sand and salt flats burned under the sun. The tallest things between the men and the distant mountains were a few sickly mesquite trees and creosote bushes. But most of the land was owned by the Government and could be settled on without cost. The lure of free land and the promise of water "coming soon" drew people in by the thousands.

On May 14, 1901, the first red rush of water from the Colorado flowed through the feeder canals and within a few weeks the crops began to grow. The word spread and thousands more farmers flocked to the Imperial Valley. By 1904, 7,000 men and their families worked their own land happily. The Southern Pacific Railroad laid tracks into the Valley itself in order to carry new settlers in and farm produce out. Dozens of little towns sprung up, including one right on the Mexican border. The Mexican half of this town became known as Mexicali and the California side was called Calexico.

By this time everyone was making money. The farmers sold $700,000 worth of crops in 1904. The company owned by Rockwood and Chaffey charged the farmers $22 per acre to supply them with water, and had taken in more than $2 million. Even the Southern Pacific Railroad had bought land on the Mexican side of the border in the hope that it, too, could be irrigated and become valuable farm land.

Perhaps Chaffey knew that the Imperial Valley boom was headed for trouble. Or perhaps he was tired of running an irrigation business. Whatever his reasons were, he sold his interest in the water company to a group of men and left the Valley for good.

Almost as soon as he was gone, problems began to appear. The muddy water of the Colorado had dropped tons of sediment into the channel that Chaffey had built to water the dry riverbed. As the canal slowly choked with sediment, the flow of water into the Valley slowed and the crops began to die in the 100-degree heat.

Rockwood and his new partners looked for a way to open the channel. They decided that removing the plug of silt would take too long, so they dug a small ditch to connect the main irrigation canal with the river around the plug. They did not build a gate with which they could control the flow of water through the ditch because it was February. Everyone felt certain that they would be safe from high water until the snows melted in the spring. By then, surely the main channel would be cleared.

But the Colorado River did not cooperate with the people of Imperial Valley. High in the mountains, rain fell and snow melted. The Colorado ran bank-full toward the Gulf of California. With no flood gate to stop it, much of this water left the river and flowed through the temporary ditch, through the old riverbed, into Imperial Valley.

Rockwood was in Los Angeles when word reached him that water was rushing out of control through the irrigation canals. He hurried back to the Valley and found that the water had widened the new ditch to 60 feet. Twice he tried to close the break with dams of brush, logs, and sandbags. But both times the rushing, red flood tore the materials away. That was in March, 1905.

By June, the ditch had become 160 feet wide and 90,000 cubic feet of water was pouring into the basin each second. The water found its way through the irrigation ditches and across the new farmland to the deepest part of the Valley. There it began to collect and spread, forming a lake that later would be known as the Salton Sea. The helpless settlers watched the lake grow larger and larger, covering more and more farmland. If the flow of water into the Valley was not stopped, they realized, the entire basin might become one huge lake.

Farmers must have wished for rowboats such as this one being used during a Kansas City flood.

Rockwood's water company was rapidly going broke paying for the debris that was being thrown into the water only to be carried away by the current. In desperation, the owners of the company asked the Southern Pacific Railroad for help.

The managers of the railroad wanted to help stop the flood for several reasons. The success of the farmers in the Valley would provide the railroad with a lot of business, hauling produce to New Orleans and bringing people and supplies into the Valley. Also the railroad owned a huge tract of land in the desert just across the border in Mexico and this land could someday be turned into valuable farmland with water from the Imperial Valley irrigation system. And, of course, the railroad had laid a lot of tracks through the valley and, as the

Salton Sea spread, these were being covered and had to be rebuilt elsewhere.

E. H. Harriman, President of the Southern Pacific Railroad, agreed to help. But he insisted on having control of the water in return for the money that it would take to control the flood. Rockwood and his friends agreed to this, and Harriman appointed a new man to head the water company. He was a civil engineer named Espes Randolph. Rockwood became the company's chief engineer. A former teacher of engineering, H. T. Cory, became Rockwood's assistant.

Together the three men tried to stop the flow of the river. They found that the Colorado no longer flowed across the delta to the Gulf of California. Instead, all of the water in the river now flowed into the Imperial Valley through the widened ditch and the old riverbed. By the fall of 1905, the Salton Sea covered 150 square miles of the basin's floor and was growing daily.

The men spent $60,000 of the railroad's money building another dam across the break in the river's bank. This dam had to be 600 feet long to reach across the ditch and it took almost all of the month of November to complete building it. Then, on the last day of November, a flash-flood smashed down the Gila River from somewhere in central Arizona. The Gila enters the Colorado River at Yuma, a short distance upstream from where the new dam had been built. The water in the larger river rose ten feet in ten hours and the new dam crumpled like paper under the pressure. More than 100,000 cubic feet of water poured through the gap each second for the next few hours, and when the water finally returned to its normal flow, no sign of the new dam could be found.

The three engineers—Rockwood, Randolph, and Cory—decided that a dam across the ditch was not possible and looked for other solutions. Rockwood showed them the original canal that had been choked with silt. He suggested that they design and build a huge, steam-driven dredge that could be used to remove the sediment from the canal. They could then build a new flood gate where the canal left the river. Once the flow of water from the river was turned into the original canal, the flow through the newer ditch would be smaller and could be dammed.

The other men agreed and the three went to San Francisco. There they found a company that could build a dredge that would do the job. Satisfied, they returned to the river to begin work on the new flood gate and wait for the delivery of the dredge, which had been promised by early summer.

It was early on the morning of April 18, 1906, in San Francisco. Many of the city's nearly 500,000 people were beginning to stir from their night's sleep. A few miles away, the rocks along the sides of a huge crack in the earth known as the San Andreas Fault shifted a few feet. Shock waves traveled out through the earth at two-miles-per-second and smashed through the city. For 75 seconds the earth shook and buildings collapsed on helpless people.

When the dust cleared, the survivors of the terri-

Sometimes the money source itself is flooded as in this Kansas City bank.

ble earthquake found thousands of buildings lying in piles of rubble and hundreds of fires springing up all over San Francisco. Firemen trying to fight these fires discovered that the tremors in the earth had destroyed the water mains. The fires spread from block to block.

The waterfront was especially hard hit, both by the earthquake itself and by fires which burned unchecked there for 48 hours. The company that was building Rockwood's dredge was ruined beyond recovery and the dredge was completely destroyed. When this news reached Rockwood, he abandoned his dream of making the desert fertile and resigned from the company.

The Southern Pacific Railroad and Espes Ran-dolph were now in complete control of the Imperial Valley water company. They were also completely responsible for the saving of the farms in the Valley. Randolph rushed to San Francisco to talk with President Harriman in the railroad's main office.

Harriman was faced with a tremendous job. His railroad had been badly damaged by the earthquake. Millions of dollars worth of trains, tracks, and buildings lay in total ruin, yet he knew that the victims of the catastrophe would rely upon the railroad for transportation out of the destroyed city and that those people who remained behind would need food and supplies that only the railroad could carry. In spite of this, he told Randolph to spend as much as another $250,000 on the flood in the Imperial Valley.

Cory, the former engineering teacher, was now in full charge of the work on the river. The late-spring floods, caused by the melting of the mountain snow, had started all along the Colorado and the Gila. Six billion cubic feet of water per day poured into the Valley through the break that was now half a mile wide. The Salton Sea in the northern end of the Valley covered an area of 400 square miles with water that was 60 feet deep in places, and it grew seven inches deeper each day. The twin towns of Calexico and Mexicali, sitting on the border at the southern end of the Valley, were three-fourths destroyed. Twelve thousand people were making preparations to abandon their farms forever.

Cory was determined to dam the flood once and for all this time. He and his friends had under-estimated the strength of the flood before, so he laid his plans carefully. During the summer of 1906, the engineer gathered materials and men. As the spring floods slowed and the flow of water dropped, he built a trestle across the ditch. On this bridge he then laid railroad tracks. Tons and tons of rock were dug from every quarry within 400 miles of the Valley and loaded into huge side-dump railroad cars.

By August, everything was ready and Cory or-dered the fourth attempt to dam the flood to begin. Three hundred of the dump cars, each carrying 60 tons of rock, rolled onto the trestle in train after train. The rocks were dumped over the side of the bridge and the dam grew quickly. The water flow-ing into the Imperial Valley slowed, became a trickle, and then stopped entirely.

Cory immediately went to work on the building of a huge flood gate, through which he could let a small amount of water flow into the valley. The farmers were happy that the flood had been stopped, but everyone knew that the farms could survive only if a steady flow of water for irrigation could be brought into the basin.

On October 11th, however, the Colorado River again reached flood stage. Cory stood on high ground above his dam and watched two-thirds of it and the new concrete flood gate lift upward on the current and wash away. For the next two weeks, more trains crossed the trestle that had somehow managed to withstand the first rush of water. Every engine in southern California and Arizona was sent to bring long trains of side-dump cars full of rock across the bridge. Most of the rock dumped into the swirling water washed away before it hit the bottom, but some remained and finally, on November 4, the dam was again solid.

This time, Cory did not stop pouring rocks into the ditch. By early December, the dam was high and strong, and ready for anything the Colorado could throw against it.

And the river tried. On December 7 a rush of water from the Gila River hit the dam furiously but could not move it. The water rushed southward across the delta, toward the Gulf.

But once on the soft silt of the delta, the tumbling water had something it could move. Steadily the current cut into the bank of the river south of the huge pile of rock. The course of the river slowly shifted to the west. A levee a half a mile south of Cory's dam was demolished and the water again broke from its banks. This time it cut a channel around the dam and found its way back into the ditch. Within a few hours, water was again flooding into the Valley through a break nearly 1,000 feet wide.

The Southern Pacific Railroad had spent nearly $2 million trying to stop the Colorado from flooding the Imperial Valley and the directors of the company decided that the Federal Government should help. Telegrams flashed back and forth between San Francisco and Washington. President Theodore

Roosevelt was uncertain that the Federal Government had any business helping a railroad stop a flood without the permission of Congress. And Congress was about to take its Christmas vacation. President Roosevelt finally promised that when Congress returned to work he would ask for some money to reimburse the railroad for the expense of fighting this new flood. So, Cory was told to go back to work trying to dam the new break.

By now the engineer knew that it was possible to dam the flow from the river, if he could get enough rock into the channel. This time two trestles were built across the new break, and rails were laid on them. Rock was again hauled in, this time from as far away as 500 miles. When everything was ready, the dumping began. In the next 15 days, 3,000 of the huge side-dump cars rolled onto the bridges, dumped their 60-ton loads, and moved on.

This new pile of rock held and attention could turn again to the damage that the two years of floods had caused in the valley. The Salton Sea now covered 450 square miles of the basin floor. Deep gullies had been cut through many of the farms that had just begun to produce crops and the steady wind was again beginning to pile up the loose soil into huge dunes. Roads and railroad tracks lay under tons of loose rock and dirt. Loose boards on hundreds of deserted shacks rattled in the wind while buzzards wheeled overhead.

In Washington, President Roosevelt kept his promise and asked Congress to pay the Southern Pacific Railroad for the work they had done. At

A farm in the Imperial Valley lies drowned in water from the rampaging Colorado River.

first Congress did not want to make what was called "a gift to a private company," but later $700,000 was paid to the railroad that had spent something over $3 million to fight the flood.

A few years later, the farmers of the Valley voted to form their own water company and bought the entire canal system. From this sale, the Southern Pacific Railroad received about $3 million and, therefore, recovered the money it had spent.

In 1936 work was finished on Hoover Dam, many miles upstream on the Colorado, not far from Grand Canyon. This dam, one of the highest in the world, finally had tamed the Colorado River. Now a steady flow of water is released daily from the dam. Downstream to the south, near the site of the old canal, stand the flood gates that protect the entrance to an irrigation canal built in 1940. Through the All-American Canal, as it is called, water flows to the irrigation feeder canals in the Imperial Valley. This newer irrigation system has finally turned the once-dry desert into a half a million acres of the most productive and beautiful farm land in America.

But to the north of these fertile acres lies a quiet reminder of those terrible two years of 1905 to 1907. Without an outlet to the ocean, the Salton Sea is still nearly 30 miles long and 10 miles wide and slowly evaporates in the hot desert sun.

BUFFALO HOLLOW 1972

AMON FINLEY HAD LIVED in the Appalachian Mountain valley known as Buffalo Hollow almost all of his life. An attack of polio at the age of three months had left him partly paralyzed. Because of this he did not work in the mines that dotted the sides of the hollow. With the help of a monthly check of $136 from his dead father's Social Security and through doing as much work as his crippled arm and leg would allow, he had managed to provide for his elderly mother and pay off most of the loans on two small houses.

The houses stood in the mining camp known as Lundale. The mountains crowded in close to the camp, forcing the houses into a single row between the road and the railroad tracks. Across the narrow blacktop road, perhaps 50 yards from Amon's front door, was the quiet little stream called Buffalo Creek.

Behind his houses were two of the many mines in the valley. These were both owned by the Amherst Coal Company. The entrances to the shafts were somewhere high up on the steep side of the mountain, lost in the thick trees. A long conveyor belt ran straight down the side of the mountain to the processing plant on the valley floor. These plants, called "tipples," formed a familiar jumble of corrugated sheet iron, wires, ladders, and dirty grey smoke. Railroad cars almost always stood under the huge buildings, waiting to take on their loads of washed and sorted coal. Trains made up of 50 or more coal cars constantly traveled up and down the tracks behind Amon's houses, winding their way like huge black snakes through the nearly 20 miles of the hollow.

Even though Amon did not work for the coal company, he recognized the importance of the fossil fuel. West Virginia had for 40 years been the country's number one coal-producing state and only during the last year had it lost the championship to Kentucky. The coal deposits of Buffalo Hollow lay in the heart of Logan County, one of the main coal-producing areas in West Virginia.

Except for the little town of Man, standing at the mouth of the hollow where Buffalo Creek ran into the large Guyondot River, everything in the valley depended upon the coal mines. Not counting the 1,500 or so people who lived in Man, there were nearly 5,000 people living in 16 mining camps in Buffalo Hollow. This was more than the number of people who lived in the county seat of Logan, some 15 miles downstream on the Guyondot River.

Five hundred people were crowded into the camp of Lundale, and these were the people that Amon Finley called his neighbors. The Amherst Coal Company owned the only large buildings in the camp—two office buildings and a company store. The coal company even ran the only gasoline station in the camp.

In the 12 miles between Lundale and Man, were 11 separate mining camps. In these 11 communities lived 3,850 people. In the six miles of the valley that lay above Amon's houses there were only three camps—Lorado, Pardee, and Saunders. Lorado was the largest of the three, with a population of about 500. Pardee and Saunders were small camps of only about 100 people each. At the head of the valley, some seven miles above Lundale, stood the tipple of the Buffalo Mining Company.

Two generations of men had taken coal from the mines at the end of Buffalo Hollow. During the years of World War II, when coal had been needed more than it is today, the mines had been owned by the Lorado Coal Mining Company. The old shaft mines could not produce coal quickly enough for the steel furnaces that were busily making tanks and ships for use in the war, so the company began to strip mine the hills at the very top of the valley.

To do this, it was necessary to remove tons of slate and other useless rock in order to uncover the beds of valuable coal. The miners call this useless rock *slag*. To get the slag out of the way it was dumped into a small valley that runs into Buffalo Hollow near its head. Huge piles of the loose rock soon filled one part of the smaller valley and the tributary stream began to back up, forming a long lake. Unlike a cement dam, this slag heap had no valves that could be used to gradually release water into the stream below.

After the war, the mines were bought by the Buffalo Mining Company. By this time, the lake behind

The Buffalo Hollow flood was unusual, but Johnstown, Pennsylvania, has had a series of them. These engravings were done in 1889.

the slag dam had grown very large. In addition to water from streams, it was also made up of water that had seeped into mine shafts and had to be pumped out. By 1972, an estimated 360,000 gallons of water were being pumped into the lake from the mines. And, because the strip mining had taken so many trees from the steep hillsides, more and more water flowed into the lake along the surface of the ground.

Amon Finley had never visited the lake, but some of his neighbors had. There were actually three lakes at the head of the valley, they told him. There were two small lakes near the road and a large one farther back up the valley. The large lake stood quite a distance from the Buffalo Mine tipple, and no one really knew exactly how big it was. The slag dam that held back the large lake had grown steadily through the years until it now stood well over 100 feet high in the middle. A few people in the valley had managed to get boats into the lake and had reported that in some places the winding arms of water ran for several miles back into the mountains.

Some of the teenagers of Buffalo Hollow tried to swim in the lake but soon gave it up. The water was sour with the sulfuric acid that formed when the coal was washed, and only a few feet below the surface the water was black and thick with coal dust. Besides, they said, the lake was terribly deep. No one was able to hold his breath long enough to find the bottom.

Many people who lived in the narrow hollow below the lake were afraid that the dam might break some day. Warnings that this was going to happen were common, but in more than 30 years the dam had not broken, and so very few people were really concerned. Amon Finley hardly ever thought about the lake. His mother had died around the middle of January and the crippled man was trying now to rebuild his life. After so many years of taking care of his mother, he found that he suddenly had little to do. Much of his time was spent repairing the house she had lived in, in the hopes that he could rent it to someone.

He woke up early on the morning of Saturday, February 26, 1972. At about seven o'clock he went out to inspect the new porch he had just built. It was the biggest porch in all of Lundale—18 feet long and 12 feet wide. It was made of four-inch-thick concrete, reinforced with steel rods. He was proud of his work and was glad that the winter weather had warmed up enough to let him finish the job.

The mountains in the southern part of West Virginia had been covered by snow for much of the winter, but now all of that was suddenly gone. A few days before, the temperature had climbed up and up until it almost felt like spring. A lot of warm rain had fallen, but not enough to concern the people of Buffalo Hollow.

People living farther downstream were more concerned about the rain. The Guyondot River was running bank-full at Man and had topped the 26-foot-deep mark on the bridges at Logan the day before. This was more than five feet below the record set in 1963, but it was bad enough. The lower two streets of Logan's business section were badly flooded, roads and bridges were awash, and the schools had been dismissed early for the weekend.

One man knew how big the lake above the hollow was and that the warm rain had washed the melting snow from the mountainsides into the lake. He was Deputy Sheriff Otto Mutters. A phone call at 5:30 on Saturday morning started him on his way up the hollow. The report was that the water behind the big dam was within a foot of the top of the slag pile. Mutters knew that the loose rock could not stand for long if the water started running over the top. He drove to the mine tipple at the head of the hollow. An official of the mine there told him that the dam was in good shape, but Mutters was not convinced. For the next two hours the deputy drove up and down the hollow, warning the people there that the dam might break. But few of them listened to him.

"I didn't know how much water was up there," Amon Finley explained later. "If I had known, I'd have got out right then."

Other people tried to warn Amon and his neighbors. At 7:10 a.m., an employee of the mining company took a look at the dam and called his mother on the two-way radio in his truck.

"The dam is going to go," he warned her. "Get out of there now and warn as many people as you can."

The woman quickly gathered up what she could and left for the safety of the hillside. She passed the warning on to her next door neighbor, who in turn passed it on to Amon as he stood admiring his new front porch. But the man still did not believe that he was in any danger and went back into his house.

Other employees of the mining company had realized that the dam was in dangerous condition. A group of them decided at about 7:00 a.m. that the valley should be evacuated. They formed a long parade of cars and began making their way down from the mine, blowing their horns and flashing their lights.

Just below the dam stood the cluster of houses called Saunders. At a couple of minutes after 8:00 a.m., the electricity went off and someone shouted a warning.

"Run for your lives!"

But there wasn't time for most of the people of Saunders. From their houses they watched helplessly as the small dam that held back the lake nearest them gave way. They heard a terrible roar as 20 million cubic feet of water pushed through the narrow opening. A church was wrenched from its foundations and floated toward them. A wall of water from the large dam farther up the valley topped the smaller dams and crushed the houses like toys.

Cars streamed in all directions as the desperate people tried to get to higher ground. One family spent precious minutes trying to catch their dog and the water was waist deep before they finally got to their car. A man with only one leg lost first one crutch and then the other in the swirling water and finally had to crawl up the steep hillside. A car bounced down the railroad tracks in an effort to get closer to the side of the mountain. The water stripped the bedrock bare of soil as it roared through the mining camp.

The water wiped out the few houses of Saunders and smashed through Pardee without warning. This camp was wiped clean of everything but the biggest cottonwood trees. By this time the flood was a wall of tumbling, black water nearly 40 feet high, bouncing from wall to wall of the valley. Fortunately for the people farther down the hollow, the valley floor is not steep and the thick water moved down it at what must have been only about 20 miles an hour.

The homes of the 500 people living at Lorado were demolished next. Railroad tracks were torn from their ties and bent double. Railroad cars of coal, weighing more than 50 tons, were rolled like toys in a bathtub.

The torrent rushed down on Lundale. In spite of the warnings that he had gotten, Amon Finley was back in his house, standing near a second story window. He heard a roaring sound, and looked up the valley.

"It looked like a big, old, black wall coming," he said later. "I could see that it was carrying houses along with it."

As fast as his crippled leg would carry him, he rushed down the stairs and out of the house. Without thinking, he gathered up the jacket he had thrown on a chair near the front door. He ran down the valley, away from the tumbling water, around the side of a neighbor's house, across the railroad tracks, and scrambled up the steep slope to safety.

"The water was right behind me all the way. I usually can't run very fast, but I'll tell you that I was really moving that day!"

From the side of the mountain, Amon looked back into his valley. The black water seemed to pick up his houses and toss them into the air. Then the

Heavy rainfall is often responsible for rivers going over their banks and flooding the surrounding land. This photograph, taken in 1877, shows a flooded area of Richmond, Virginia, on the banks of the James River.

wall of water poured over them and smashed them to bits. The heavy cement porch that he had worked on for so long lifted in the current like a raft and floated downstream. His prize apple trees bent with the force of the water and then were ripped out by the roots. A telephone pole snapped like a twig.

The 12-year-old son of a family that lived a few houses down from Amon had been playing in the back of an old pickup truck. The truck was parked in the lot near the company store in Lundale. The boy looked up and saw the water coming. Realizing what had happened, he started to run for the mountainside. But then he remembered his mother and father at home, and knew that they did not know that they were in danger. Quickly he ran back up the valley, directly toward the black wall of water. Wading through water up to his knees, he managed to warn his parents in time for them all to escape. But their home and everything in it was washed away.

At the camp called Stowe, a family heard the noise and saw what looked to them to be a huge cloud rolling down the valley. Without taking time to put on shoes, they left the house and plunged into water that was up to their knees. While they struggled through the water, their house was torn apart and from the safety of a hill side they watched their car being lifted up and thrown onto the pile of rubble that had been their home.

Here, at the place where Stowe stood, the valley begins to widen out. You might expect that the

water would have spread out here and lost much of its force. But a metal bridge, its sign announcing that it could hold a weight of 12,000 pounds, was torn from its foundations and carried downstream for several yards. There it stuck, and tons of broken houses, cars, and bodies piled up behind it.

At Crites, the valley narrows again, and here the water swept all signs of life away. Then it spilled out into another broad place in the valley. By the time it reached Amhersdale, the mid-point in the valley, the flood was nearly 500 yards across and still 20 feet deep. The main current of the river was strong enough to carry away or damage 32 of 37 houses standing alongside the creek bed, but the water killed very few people below this point. And, by the time it reached Man, the flood did not damage strong buildings at all. But it carried tons of black mud into almost every home and building. Many of these had to be abandoned later because the walls were full of the slimy silt.

Back in the hollow, the people began coming down out of the mountains. Amon Finley returned to Lundale to find that nothing remained of his two houses, not even the foundations. Uninsured against flood, his life savings of $18,000 were gone. Worse than this, the bodies of his neighbors lay sprawled in the mud and hung from the trees in all directions. Those who had survived felt thankful to be alive, even though they owned nothing but the clothing they wore. The rain suddenly began to feel quite cold. Except for the company store and one other building, Lundale was gone.

Buffalo Hollow

Help began to arrive quickly. Rescue teams from Man began walking up the hollow almost as soon as the splintered wreckage reached the town. Helicopters fluttered over the ruined hollow, and police cars sat sideways across the road, their red lights reflecting on the piles of debris.

It was Sunday before Amon Finley was taken aboard a helicopter. The clattering machine flew first to the head of the valley to pick up two more survivors from the wreckage of Saunders. From the air, Amon looked down on the smashed valley.

For the only time in his life he saw the dams—three piles of black gravel, each with a huge hole torn from its center. He saw the valley floor littered with the wreckage of hundreds of homes, smashed cars, overturned railroad cars, and twisted railroad tracks. He watched men scramble up the sides of the mountains, trying to reach the bodies that sometimes hung 30 feet above the now-quiet stream. And everywhere he saw that everything was covered with a black slime that would later dry into a thick layer of coal dust.

The helicopter took its passengers down the valley and landed on the football field of Man High School. The pilot told the three to report to the Red Cross center in the field house. There they found many people ready to help them find temporary shelter, warm clothing, and something to eat.

The town was already full of soldiers. Troop I of the West Virginia National Guard had been called into action and had taken over the problem of searching the valley for survivors. Nearly 1,500 people were reported as missing, and a steady stream of trucks and helicopters brought bodies to the temporary morgue set up in the Plainview Grade School.

The need for food and drinkable water farther up the hollow was becoming a serious problem. In the ruins of Lorado, more than 500 people had gathered and needed help. Another 500 workers had come into the valley, and these people also needed food and water. Huge, double-rotared helicopters of the U. S. Army soon began to carry heavy freight into the hollow. Water purification units were flown in from the U. S. Army post at Ft. Bragg, North Carolina. Salvation Army mobile kitchens from as far away as Washington, D. C., were seen handing out free food in the ruins of three camps.

Groups of Mennonites from Virginia and Pennsylvania began to arrive by the carload. Trained by the Virginia flood of 1969, these volunteers quickly organized themselves into search-and-rescue teams.

On Monday, seven more bodies were dug from the debris and added to the 60 people who already lay in the morgue. The names of 250 missing people were posted throughout the valley and appeared in every newspaper in the state. Relatives of the missing fearfully inspected each body as it was brought into the morgue.

On Wednesday the body of a woman was found in the Guyondot River nearly 100 miles downstream from the broken dams. She was covered with the slimy, black mud that stained everything in Buffalo Hollow. This discovery brought the total of known dead to 72.

Heavy earthmoving equipment was now being brought into the hollow. Bulldozers, front-end loaders, trucks, and tractors probed the debris and moved tons of dirt and rocks. A steady rain poured down on the rescue teams, but the temperature was warm during the daylight hours. From the smashed houses piled against the bridge at Stowe, the Mennonites pulled the bodies of two small children. By Saturday morning, a full week after the dam burst, 85 bodies had been found and 120 people were still missing. No one dared guess what the final death toll would be.

It seemed that the hollow was beginning to recover somewhat. A path had been pushed through the debris to the very end of the valley, roughly following the course of the old road. None of the bridges were still standing, of course, but the bed of Buffalo Creek had been cleared and trucks could easily ford it when it was necessary. Piles of debris had been carefully searched and were burning in a chilly March wind. Seven Salvation Army canteens served food and drinks to the hundreds of people who worked in spite of the cold rain. Mobile homes owned by the U. S. Government had begun to arrive and electric power was again available to the lower parts of the valley.

By the end of another week it looked as if Buffalo Hollow would quickly return to normal. The National Guard troops had left. The mines as far

A dam does not have to break to cause flooding. Here on the plains of Kansas rain fell for 53 days, from mid-May to mid-July in 1951. The smaller rivers soon overflowed their banks and the flood waters swept into Manhattan, Kansas, on the banks of the Kansas River, so quickly businessmen had to be taken out by boats. More than half the town was under five feet of water, electric power and telephones were out, and thousands of people were left homeless.

up the valley as Lorado had started operations again and many of the men were able to bring home regular paychecks. Three hundred people were still without homes, but the Government officials promised that mobile homes would arrive before the end of the month. No more bodies were being found, in spite of the fact that 51 people were still reported missing. The Mennonites were again busy carrying mud from the houses that still stood, and the sounds of their hammers and saws filled the cold air.

But something went wrong. Buffalo Hollow did not return to normal. A year and a half later the scars of the flood were still to be seen everywhere. The road above Lorado was still not repaired. People still lived in Government-owned mobile homes and only a few houses were being built to replace those destroyed by the water.

Arguments as to who was responsible for the disaster went on and on. At least one national magazine called it "murder." The mining company that owned the dam claimed that the state government refused to allow them to release water from the lake. The company also claimed the flood was "an act of God."

"The State was more concerned over the welfare of the fish in the river than they were in the welfare of the people," an official of the mining company said. "Now both the fish and the people are gone. The dam simply wasn't able to hold all of the water that God put into the lake."

State officials, on the other hand, claimed that they could find no request from the mining company to release water from the lake. But apparently the State Inspectors had not looked at the dam for more than 14 months before the disaster occurred.

As the arguments went on, the people who still lived in Buffalo Hollow tried to rebuild their lives. Some left the hollow forever, of course. Others remained, but lived in constant fear. In the spring, when the heavy rains came, some mothers refused to send their children to school and fathers refused to leave their families, even to go to work. Some of the people slept in their clothes, while others sat on their porches throughout the night, watching the river.

On February 25, 1973, one year after the disaster, a memorial service was held in the Man High School Field House. Listed on the back page of the Order of Service were the names of 114 known dead. In the cemetery are four headstones marked "unknown." About 20 people were still unaccounted for.

During this memorial service, the survivors of the flood remembered the tragedy. They also tried to find something to be thankful for.

"We are not the same as we were a year ago," the Reverend Ralph Thompson said, "because we have experienced suffering, loss, sorrow, frustration, and anger which have left their marks upon us. In some ways we are stronger; in some ways we are weaker.

"We are grateful for neighbors and friends," he continued, "who have shared with us during these difficult days and who remain by our side this day."

Among the people who stayed "by the side" of the people of Buffalo Hollow were teams of workers from the Mennonite Disaster Service (MDS). Among the first of the rescuers were the black-bearded Mennonites from Virginia and Pennsylvania. Among them was Jonas Kanagy.

After the bodies were recovered and the houses cleared, another type of Mennonite began to arrive. These men and women were from Ohio, Illinois, and Indiana. Few wore the traditional dark clothing and none of the men had spade-shaped beards. These were skilled craftsmen and trained social workers, and they had come to stay until the people of Buffalo Hollow were back on their feet.

An example of this "new" type of Mennonite is Ralph Sommer, whom we met in the summer of 1973, a year and a half after the flood. He wears his graying hair long and has heavy sideburns. Instead of the beard I had come to expect, he wears a bushy mustache. Trained in social work, he works with his wife who is an experienced teacher. Also on the MDS team is a retired building contractor and 12 volunteers of high school and college age.

The eight boys and four girls who made up the summer work team came from as far away as Canada. They paid their own transportation into Logan County and received $15 per month spending money, food, and room. Most of them were

Jonas Kanagy, a Unit Leader of the Mennonite Disaster Service which was organized in 1951 to help victims of disasters. Since that time the organization has given both time and money to those in need after a disaster in the United States, Canada, and many other parts of the world.

62

Mennonites, but Sommer said that he would be happy to have any volunteer who wanted to work.

The main job of the group after the flood was the repair and rebuilding of houses. At first this was a disappointment to Sommer.

"I thought that we were going to be able to build quite a few new homes," he said. "But the state is trying to build a bigger highway through the hollow and no one wants to build a home on land that might be taken for a right-of-way.

"However, I think now that it has been good for our young people to work primarily on rebuilding. Instead of getting into only four or five homes this summer, they have been able to get into 20 or 30. This has given them a chance to learn a lot about people whose life style is very much different from their own.

"I have encouraged our young people to take the time to sit and talk with the people of the hollow. This is good for the local people. It gives them a chance to talk out their problems. And it helps our kids to understand the feelings and frustrations of others. They have come to understand themselves a little better, I think. They get to compare their own values and ideas with very much different kinds of values and ideas."

The Mennonite team lived and worked out of five mobile homes supplied free by the U. S. Government. On the other side of the trailer park was another group of young volunteers, this one sponsored by the Quakers. Working closely together, the two groups learned how to share their abilities and time with people who are in need.

"Right after the flood, it was easy to see the desperate needs of the people here," Sommer said. "It is easy to throw yourself into the job of cleaning mud out of someone's house. It is a little more difficult to understand the need that a family might have for an extra bedroom, even when there are 14 people in a house with only four rooms. Our young people have come to see that eight people sleeping in the same bedroom is a crisis, just as much as having mud in the house."

The Mennonites planned to stay in Buffalo Hollow at least through the summer of 1974, and Sommer felt that they might have to stay even longer. He saw a great need for legal aid, family guidance, and child-care centers.

"We hope to be able to work through the local churches, rather than as Mennonites. The needs of the people here are going to continue for a long, long time. We hope that we can help set up a local organization that can do the job."

FLOODS: THEIR CAUSES AND CONTROL

THROUGHOUT THE HISTORY of the earth, floods have plagued mankind. No part of the earth, except the highest land, seems to be entirely safe from floods. Even in the dryest deserts water rushes down normally dry gulleys once in a while, washing away anything that man has been foolish enough to put in its path.

In the United States alone, during an average year, 80 people are drowned in flood waters. An average of 75,000 Americans must leave their homes each year to escape floods.

As you have seen from what you have read in this book, floods may be caused by many different things. Perhaps the most common causes of floods are heavy rainfalls or deep snows that melt more quickly than normal. Dams may break and cause the valleys below them to be suddenly under water. Or a hurricane may push high storm waves across a beach and cause a flood on the land beyond. Other severe floods along the ocean shoreline may be caused by the dreaded *tsunami* waves, which in turn are caused by underwater earthquakes or volcanoes.

But often the real cause of a flood is man. Because of his desire to make money quickly or through his lack of understanding of the way nature works, man tries to change the normal course that water follows across the land. He builds dams. He changes the course of the rivers. And he builds his homes, cities, and factories in areas that are known to be in danger of flooding.

At first, it seems logical that man should settle along the flood plains of rivers, where the danger of flooding is the worse. The floods of the past have enriched the soil of the valleys by dropping tons of rich soil along either side of the river's channel. And the river itself provides water for man's use in dozens of ways—from drinking water to a free method of transportation. But the floods that have washed over the land of the river's valley will come again and again, and the cost can be tremendous.

Floods may vary greatly in size, sometimes covering only a few acres and at other times inundating millions of acres of farm land and towns. The size of the flood makes little difference to the people caught in it. To the family who has just seen everything they owned washed away, it is of little consolation to know that thousands of other people have suffered in the same way.

The most damaging floods in the United States are caused by too much rainfall. A typical flood of this type usually starts with a long period of fairly steady rain. When the rain first begins, very little of it finds its way into the streams. Instead, most of the rainfall is at first caught by the vegetation on the land and absorbed by the soil.

Venice is often called the "sinking city." The Piazza San Marco is often flooded by extremely high tides. These inhabitants are crossing the Piazza on a temporary bridge.

As the rain continues to fall, some of the water that has soaked into the soil reaches the streams through seepage. Eventually the soil becomes saturated with water and can hold no more. At this point, any rain that falls will run across the surface of the ground, downhill, and into the streams.

High in the mountains, the small streams move swiftly and cut deep-sided, V-shaped valleys. Their channels are more or less straight, turning only when they run against a large mass of rock that cannot be cut through. Flash floods along the banks of these types of streams are common, but usually do little damage, since the water is usually not deep enough to get out of the deep-sided valley.

As the water in these small streams moves down the side of the mountains it is joined by water from other streams. Eventually a river is formed. The river, running over more flat land than do the mountain streams, does not move very fast and may carve a winding path across a broad flood plain. From all over the river's watershed, a number of tributary streams may add more water into the main channel. The water in the big river grows deeper and spills over its natural banks, quickly spreading out over the flat flood plain on either side of the channel.

This fast-moving water carries with it particles of soil washed from the hillsides. When it begins to move more slowly, the soil is deposited on the flood plains. Much of the best farmland in the United States lies there in the natural flat land beside the rivers. Perhaps as much as 50 million acres of our country are flat lowlands, bordering rivers. It has been estimated that more than ten million Americans live on these plains and are therefore exposed to the dangers of floods almost anytime it rains upriver from where they live. Damage to property standing in these areas now runs into the billions of dollars each year.

Scientists, engineers, government officials, and many other people spend their lives trying to protect these people from the dangers of floods. The problem is being attacked from many different directions: control, prediction and warning, and relief and rehabilitation for the victims.

The great hope of everyone who lives in an area threatened by floods is that someday we will learn how to prevent the rivers from damaging property and people. There are many state and federal programs aimed at doing just this. There are also attempts to prevent people from building homes and living in dangerous areas. The trouble with these attempts is that the flood plains of our major rivers contain rich soil the farmer wants to own. The land along the rivers is flat and builders find it cheaper to construct buildings there than in the mountains. With water nearby, the manufacturer finds it profitable to put factories on the flood plain. Thus, it is difficult to keep people out of these potentially dangerous areas.

Other programs set up standards for construction of buildings in areas that might flood. Ways are being found to build houses and larger buildings so that they will not easily float off their foundations during a flood. Electric wires and appliances can be made in such ways that they will not be damaged by being submerged. Waterproof coverings for windows and doors are being made, and these can be installed to protect a building during flood times. Buildings on huge cement pillars are now seen in some flood plains, with their offices high above possible flood depths.

Throughout the history of civilized man, attempts have been made to prevent the rivers from leaving their channels. The construction of levees, dikes, flood walls, and the like is the most common way this has been done. In all parts of the world, large rivers are lined with high, man-made walls of dirt, sandbags, and cement. Levees help solve the problem somewhat, but they create other problems. Holding a flooding river inside high levees increases the speed of the water and this, in turn, causes the water to erode away the banks of the river at a faster rate. And, when a levee is overtopped, the result is a sudden flooding of the low land behind the wall, sometimes without warning to the people living there.

Another method of preventing the river from leaving its channel is to make the natural riverbed wider, deeper, and straighter. At first, this seems to work fairly well, especially when combined with a system of levees. However, once a riverbed has been made bigger and straighter, it is usually necessary to continue to dredge sediment from it. This can be a very costly method of flood control and one that must be continued forever.

Have you ever gone camping and dug a ditch around your tent? This is an example of a third way of preventing rivers from flooding. The idea here is to give the flood waters another channel to run into before it can flood into an area inhabited by people. There are several such alternate channels along the Mississippi River. When the river becomes dangerously full of water, the extra water can be channeled through other stream beds which relieves the threat of flood farther downstream.

Huge dams have been built all over the world in attempts to prevent floods. The dams block the natural flow of the rivers and hold their water in huge lakes. Thus, when a heavy flow of water comes down the river, it can be held and released at a later time. The lakes behind such dams have other values beyond their use in flood control. We use many of these lakes for recreational areas, water supplies for towns and industries, and for irrigation of farm lands below the dams. The water rushing through openings at the base of the dam can also be used to generate electricity. There are problems, of course. Sediment that normally would have flowed on down the river collects behind these dams and eventually fills up the lake. And, the building of such dams must result in the permanent drowning of many acres of farm and woodlands. Too, there is always the possibility that the dam will break and cause tremendous flooding downstream.

The last method of trying to prevent flood water from leaving the river channel is careful management of the land in the river's watershed. Since much of the water that enters the river came to it over the surface of the land, scientists have tried to find ways to lower the amount of runoff. One way to do this is to keep the soil carefully planted with a heavy cover of vegetation. Another way is to build small ponds to catch and hold the heavy runoff of water. In these ways, the water is held until it can soak into the soil, rather than run off into the streams.

But in spite of all of these programs, rivers continue to flood and people continue to suffer. In order to protect us from damaging floods it is necessary that floods be predicted and that warnings be sent out to people who may be in their paths.

The prediction of floods is a highly scientific business. It begins with the National Weather Service and the scientists who study the weather. Using highly complicated equipment, such as airplanes, radar, and satellites, these scientists watch the weather all over the world. Using the data they gather, the weather men try to predict when and where it will rain and how much water will fall.

Engineers who have studied the flood patterns of a particular river basin watch the river carefully. Measurements are made of the water level all along the length of the river, from the mountain streams to the ocean.

Forecasts of what the river might do are carefully prepared. If it appears that the river might reach its flood stage, warnings are sent out. Such warn-

Above: Using rowboats, rescue workers aid stranded citizens in Kansas City, Kansas, during a flood in 1951.
Below: Helicopters are often used to survey flood damage and search for people in need of help.

Florence, Italy, once had a flood that destroyed many invaluable records and art objects. A scene from the National Library where hundreds of students spent long hours digging through the mud and slime for the many old and priceless manuscripts stored there.

ings, if accurate, can save many lives and allow people time to move valuable property to safer ground.

But the science of weather and flood forecasting is not 100 percent accurate, and some floods do catch people unaware. Even when there is enough warning, many people do not leave the threatened area. Or, if they do leave, they often must leave their property behind.

In every flood there are victims who are in need of relief and rehabilitation. After a flood strikes, the first need of the people in the damaged area is to be rescued from the flood water. People are often stranded in the upper floors of their homes, on the roofs of buildings, on hills that have become islands, or even in the branches of trees or the cross-arms of telephone poles. While the flood is still raging it is necessary for other people to come to the rescue of these stranded victims. Since this need comes early in the flood, it is usually up to local people to do this rescue work. Fire and police departments, civil defense units, military units, and individuals go out in boats and helicopters to save these lives.

Even before the water reaches a community many people will have heard the warnings and moved from their homes. As the water rises, more and more displaced people will join the first refugees. These people must find shelter, food, water, and sometimes clothing. If the weather is bad, these necessities must be supplied quickly. Children and old people have special needs that must be met. Early in the disaster the problems must be handled by local organizations, such as civil defense or local church groups. Later such organizations as the Red Cross and Salvation Army may help.

After the water level drops, someone must wade through the mud and debris in order to search for the dead and injured. Bodies must be taken to a morgue, identified, and buried. The injured must be gotten to hospitals quickly and safely. It is up to local people—people who know the damaged area well—to coordinate these search-and-rescue operations. But much of the actual work may be taken over by people from the outside. Teams of Mennonites may arrive. Rescue squads, firemen, and policemen from nearby communities often come to help. National Guardsmen and military personnel are usually on their way as soon as word of the disaster is received. But someone from civil defense or the local police must be able to direct the work of these volunteers. And some groups, such as the Red Cross, the Salvation Army, or local organizations must provide food and shelter for these workers.

Throughout the flood, the workmen of the local utility companies and the local government are busy trying to restore electric power, telephone service, and fuel supplies. Within a few days after flood waters subside, the bodies of the dead and the injured have to be removed from the debris and attention given to damaged property. Work then must begin on cleaning and rebuilding the homes and businesses caught by the water. The owners of the property may be able to do this for themselves, but often they are too shocked by the experience they have been through to be able to help themselves. Usually it is necessary for someone from the

Unusual heavy rains cause rivers to overflow their banks and flood the surrounding areas. These cars were left in their parking places on the city street; presumably the owners waded onto higher ground for safety.

outside to come in and help them get started. They not only need help in carrying out the mud and rebuilding their buildings, they also need money. If their homes are too badly damaged, it is sometimes necessary to buy materials for new ones.

If a disaster has been a large one, a great number of state and federal agencies, local organizations, and national relief groups will be available to help. Low-interest loans and rent-free mobile homes may be supplied by the federal government. Mudding-out and rebuilding is usually done by such groups as the Mennonite Disaster Service, working under the direction of the Red Cross. Local and state governments can supply help in various forms.

Sooner or later the Red Cross and the Salvation Army move on to new disaster sites, and the officers of the U.S. government agencies leave. But the people of the destroyed area will still need help. Perhaps their local industries have been badly damaged and many people are out of work. Sometimes people develop mental illnesses because of the experiences they have had and are in need of professional help. Often children are orphaned and need to be cared for. And many times, so much valuable property has been destroyed that the area cannot afford to pay the taxes necessary to rebuild its schools, roads, and water and sewer systems.

You may never be caught in a flood, but over the next 50 years some four million Americans will be. An understanding of floods, their causes and prevention, may help you to save the life of one of these people.

TRAGEDY AT THE KNICKERBOCKER THEATER

THE MAN HAD JUST FINISHED feeding the lions when he saw the two people coming toward him. The two dim figures wading through the snowdrifts were about all that he could see—it was snowing so hard he had trouble seeing anything else. Both of them were dressed in khaki clothing, tall leather boots, and had broad brimmed hats pulled down over their eyes.

"Hello, there!" one of the people called to him. "Can you tell us how to get out of the park?"

"Can you believe it?" the other person said, laughing. "We are lost in a snowstorm in the middle of the Washington zoo!" It was a woman's voice, and the words were spoken with a heavy European accent.

The zoo keeper gave the couple directions and watched as they trudged off. Dick Richardson held his wife's hand to keep her from slipping in the deep snow.

"It's getting dark," he said. "Time to go home, Bob."

"I wish you wouldn't call me *Bob*. That's a silly name for a girl."

"I know," he said, laughing. "But who can pronounce your real name?"

"Boukje is a perfectly good name," she insisted. "I know a lot of women named Boukje."

"In the Netherlands, perhaps," her husband replied. "But not in Washington, D.C."

The couple had been married for only seven months. In spite of the depression that the country was suffering through, Dick had managed to find a job as an electrical engineer. His new wife, Bob, was going to school and also worked part-time at the Embassy of the Netherlands as an interpreter and a secretary. Even with two salaries, they had little money. Because of this, they were living with Dick's parents.

"I wonder if the Nelsons have arrived. Perhaps the snow kept them home."

"I doubt it, Bob. They could easily walk. And the way my parents like to play cards, I expect they insisted that they come, even in this snow."

It had been snowing in Washington for nearly 24 hours. Everything in the city was covered with a thick, wet blanket. More than two feet of heavy snow lay on the level areas. The limbs of the many trees that lined 18th Street were covered with white. The falling snow made halos around the dim bulbs in the street lights at each corner. Traffic had been stopped completely for hours, and the only sounds were the squeak of the Richardsons' shoes on the wet snow.

Even the streetcars had been stopped by the snow. Bob and Dick crossed and recrossed 18th Street, trying to find the buried tracks. But the snow was too deep.

The couple finally reached the apartment house and stamped their feet to shake the snow from their boots. They climbed the stairs and entered the door of the apartment. Four people looked up from their card game as they entered.

Bob and Dick greeted the older Richardsons and their guests. Then Bob gave a quiet signal to her husband. He followed her to the kitchen.

"Dick, I don't want to stay here while they play cards. We would be in the way. Let's go to the movies."

Dick quickly agreed. Living with his parents in the apartment was difficult for the newlyweds. They tried to avoid disturbing their parent's lives as much as they could. So they put on their coats, said goodby, and went back out into the snow.

Only four blocks away, at the corner of 18th Street and Columbia Road, stood the Knickerbocker Theater. The building was a modern one, made of brick, marble, cement and steel. The theater was only six years old. This was late January, 1922, so none of the moving picture theaters in the United States were very old. The oldest, in New York City, had been open for less than 20 years.

The picture that was being shown was called *School Days*. Along with it was a short comedy, *Get-Rich-Quick Wallingford*. Both were in black and white. There was some talk of someone trying to make a feature-length film in color, but no one in the small crowd that entered the Knickerbocker Theater that Saturday night had ever seen one.

As Dick bought the tickets, Bob looked at the

During a city blizzard the fire department is often called upon to help. A woodcut from Harper's Weekly, March 24, 1888, shows firemen struggling to answer an alarm during a blizzard. Before the age of motor cars, fire-fighting equipment was drawn by teams of horses.

Burning holes in the snow was one way of clearing city streets after a blizzard.

deserted streets. The theater was shaped almost like a triangle, fitted into the odd angle made by the intersection of Columbia Road and 18th Street. The brick wall that ran along the 18th Street side of the building was straight, but the wall facing Columbia Road was curved. This curving wall matched the curve of the road and the sidewalk.

Bob remembered that another streetcar line ran down the center of the curving Columbia Road. Huge inter-urban cars, nearly three times as heavy as regular streetcars, often ran down these tracks. She and Dick had often ridden the rattling, shaking electric cars out into the country for picnics or to visit relatives who lived in nearby towns. Now the tracks lay deeply buried. The snow had even stopped the traffic on Columbia Road.

As a matter of fact, the snow had almost paralyzed the entire city. Even the fire department equipment was having trouble getting through. The hose wagon and the pumper truck that made up Engine Company 21 were both stuck in a snow bank only two blocks from their station house on Adams Mill Road. A young fireman, named Bill Hoeke, sweated under his heavy clothing as he dug and pushed to free the trucks.

"Rough going!" one of the firemen said, straightening the kinks in his back.

"Man, that bed is going to feel good tonight!" another answered.

The four firemen and their chief, Captain T.B. Stanton, had been called out several hours before to fight a fire in a chimney only a few blocks away from their station. The fire had not been a bad one but it had been tricky, and the men were tired and dirty when they started back to the station. Because of the snow, it had taken them almost an hour to reach the driveway of the firehouse.

"This is the roughest day I *ever* had," one of the older men complained.

But, as the trucks finally rolled into the station at eight o'clock, the long, terrible night was just beginning. It was to be the worst experience any of the men in the Company would ever have.

As Bill Hoeke carefully hung up his fire-fighting coat and hat and placed his boots under them, he wondered if he had made the right decision when he joined the Washington, D.C. Fire Department He had graduated from Catholic University just a few months before with a degree in mechanical engineering. But the big depression was at its worst, and he had not been able to find a job. Since he needed work, he joined the fire department. Everyone had told him that it was a mistake. College graduates did not work as firemen in 1922. In fact, very few high school graduates took jobs as firemen back then. The job required very little knowledge of anything, much less an understanding of engineering.

But it was a steady job, and Hoeke was young and strong. During the summer months, the work had been exciting and almost fun. The winter weather had made it more difficult and much more dangerous. Hoeke often wondered, especially on Saturday when he worked for 24 hours straight, when he would be able to quit and get a decent job.

Engine Company 21 had been busy during the past week, as it always was during cold weather. Fires in chimneys and flues were common, and several houses had caught fire from open fireplaces that were still common in Washington. For several days now it had been very cold. But the sky had been clear, and the people who lived in the Nation's Capital had enjoyed skating on the frozen water of the reflecting pool in front of the Lincoln Memorial.

The cold air poured down into Washington from the north. It was pushed there by a huge high pressure area that lay over Canada. Frigid air over the northeastern United States dropped temperatures into the low 20's over Washington, D.C.

This scene is familiar and hasn't changed over the years.

To the south of Washington, off the coast of Georgia, was a low pressure area. The air in this low was warmer and contained a lot of moisture gathered up from the Atlantic Ocean. The mass of wet air slowly drifted northward.

The cold, dry air from Canada and the warm, wet air from the south met almost directly over Washington, D.C. The result was one of the heaviest snowfalls to have ever struck the Central Atlantic Coast. By Saturday afternoon, January 28, 1922, more than 25 inches of snow had fallen. This was more than twice as much snow as had ever fallen there before in a single 24-hour period.

As the Richardsons entered the theater, the comedy "short" was playing. Like all movies in 1922, it was silent. An orchestra provided music that helped set the mood of the picture. It was dark in the balcony where Bob and Dick liked to sit. They moved carefully down the aisle toward the box seats that lined the edge of the balcony.

"The man at the ticket booth said we could sit in the boxes if we wanted," Dick told his wife. "The theater has only about 200 people in it."

"Everyone must be sitting downstairs. I can see only four other people up here."

"Let's sit just in back of the box seats," Dick suggested. "I don't feel right about sitting in an expensive seat if I didn't pay for it."

Two small boys sat alone in the first row behind the box seats. The Richardsons felt their way into the row just behind them. The boys were laughing loudly at Bill Haines' antics on the screen. The couple sat down, and slowly their eyes became accustomed to the dim light.

"Move over one seat, so I can put our coats on the aisle," Dick suggested to his wife. She did not answer. He looked at her and started to speak again. But he stopped as he saw the look of horror on her face. He followed her gaze to the roof of the theater. As he did, she screamed.

A huge crack was racing across the ceiling. Plaster showered down on them. Then powdery snow blew in through the hole in the roof. With a deep rumble, the entire ceiling collapsed on the theater below.

"Get down!" Dick ordered, pushing his wife onto the floor between the seats. As he fell on top of her, the entire building shook and shivered as huge blocks of cement smashed downward.

Tons of debris fell onto the balcony. The backs of the seats kept it from crushing the Richardsons. But the weight caused the box seats and the first row to tear loose. The two boys who had been sitting just in front of the Richardsons screamed as the edge of the balcony fell onto the more than 200 people sitting on the ground floor.

The theater organist had been in the lobby of the theater trying to make a telephone call. He kept glancing at his watch as he listened to the strange tone made by the telephone. His call was not going through. In another minute or two, the comedy would be over, and it would be time for him to go to work playing music while people entered and left the theater. In disgust, he hung up the telephone receiver and opened the doors to the theater auditorium just as Bob Richardson screamed.

The organist stood in the open doorway in shocked horror. As he watched, the theater collapsed in front of him. He saw a huge chunk of cement from the ceiling smash down into the orchestra pit, killing the leader and several of the musicians. He turned and staggered into the snow-filled street.

Big cities still have their troubles during a big snowstorm. In January 1978, three young men try to dig out their car from a snowdrift during one of the worst snowstorms New York City had experienced since 1969.

Across the street stood a small shop with a light shining from its window. The organist ran through the snow toward the light. He pounded on the door and shouted. The woman who answered the door was an Italian emigrant who spoke very little English. She could not understand exactly what had happened. But she knew something horrible had frightened the man who stood shouting at her. Realizing that he could not make the woman understand him, the dazed man rushed away into the storm. The frightened woman ran into the street. She saw the fire alarm box on the pole at the corner. Not knowing what else to do, she pulled the alarm.

Bill Hoeke and the rest of Engine Company 21 had gone to bed. They had been back at the station for only an hour, but they were so tired that every man was asleep, except for the man on watch.

"Ping!"

The single stroke of the "joker bell" announced that a call was coming in from a fire box. Every man jumped from his bed. Slipping into their unlaced shoes and pulling up their suspenders, they ran for their trucks. Meanwhile, the tape punched its way out of the signal machine. The man on watch ran the tape quickly through his fingers, counting the holes that had been punched in it.

"Box 817," he called. "Box 817! Corner of 18th and Columbia Road!"

But every man in the Company knew where Box 817 was. It was only two blocks away in an area that was mostly homes and apartment houses. But near

the box were also many old buildings with oiled, wooden floors that would burn like paper. And, of course, there was the big Knickerbocker Theater.

Captain Stanton hurried his men onto their trucks. The men of Aerial Ladder Company 9 were all ready to move, the engine of their ladder truck sputtering in the cold air. The doors were being opened. Everyone hurried. Box 817 would call out four engine companies, two ladder companies and the 4th Battalion Chief. They all knew that this could be a big fire.

The hose truck of Engine Company 21 was the first to hit the snow in the street. It carried 1,200 feet of 2½-inch hose, two tanks of soda-acid chemicals that could be turned on small fires through a ¾-inch hose, and all the axes, crowbars and other tools needed by the Company. The pumper truck followed close behind the hose truck, for without the added water pressure from the pump, the hoses would be of little use against a really big fire. Third in line was the ladder-carrying truck of Company 9.

The hose truck skidded around the corner onto 18th Street. Every man searched the buildings as they passed, looking for the glow of flames. Everything seemed quiet and peaceful as they approached the Columbia Road intersection. Suddenly the front wheels of the truck struck something in the snow. The driver slammed on the brakes. Bill Hoeke jumped from the truck to see what they had hit.

"What is it, Bill?" the driver yelled through the swirling snow.

"I don't know," Hoeke shouted back. "Big metal things. They look like brass doors!" He looked around him at the buildings on the corners of the intersection. "They are the doors of the theater! There must have been an explosion in there that blew the doors clear off their hinges!"

Without waiting for orders, the men of Engine Company 21 rushed into the lobby of the building. No one was in sight. The lobby seemed normal. There was no sign of smoke or of damage from an explosion. For some strange reason, it was very, very quiet.

"Check the furnace room," Captain Stanton ordered. "It must have been the furnace."

Bill Hoeke was dragging the nozzle of the ¾-inch soda-acid line, so it was his job to search for the fire. With one other man, he hurried down a short hallway to the furnace room door. The door was slightly open with one hinge broken off. A thin wisp of smoke crept through the crack. By the light of a flashlight, the two firemen stumbled down the stairs.

The fire was a small one. The sides of the wooden coal bin were smoldering, and hot coals lay all over the floor. A single burst of soda-acid foam put the fire out, and the two men returned to the lobby. (Later Hoeke was to figure out what must have happened. The rush of air caused by the falling ceiling must have blown down the vents and into the furnace, blowing the coals out into the room.)

"No explosion down there, Captain," Hoeke reported. "Only a small fire. We took care of it. What do we have up here?"

"We don't know. Something is blocking the doors into the auditorium. We can't get them open. Here comes the Ladder Company. *Get the Johnson Door Openers!*" he shouted.

The firemen from the Ladder Truck Company quickly popped one of the doors loose and pulled it away from its frame. A pile of rubble poured through the opening and onto the lobby floor.

"Oh, my God!" someone exclaimed. "The roof has fallen in!"

The pile of debris was topped by solid blocks of cement 18 inches thick. Under this were loose pieces of cement and chunks of plaster. Steel girders could also be seen here and there. The other doors were quickly ripped from their hinges. Firemen began to dig with their bare hands into the loose rubble.

"Here's a hand!" someone shouted. "Help me dig!"

"I've got someone here!" another voice called. "I need help! Get something to dig with!"

At that moment, the Chief of the 4th Battalion arrived. He quickly surveyed the situation. He grabbed at a passing fireman.

"Pull a 2nd, 3rd, 4th and 5th alarm," he ordered. Turning to Captain Stanton, he explained, "We'll need all the men we can get. Most of the engines won't be able to get through the snow. Get to a phone and call the police. Tell them to try to find more men and equipment. Suggest that they notify the Army and the Navy. We'll need all the medical

A New York City street after the famous Blizzard of 1888 when extremely low temperatures, gale winds, and snow paralyzed the city.

help we can get, too, just in case anyone is still alive in there."

Bill Hoeke and another man had managed to dig into the loose rubble. As the tunnel grew, they took turns sliding in under the tons of cement that topped the pile of debris. One man would slide into the hole, dig away at the plaster and cement with a crow-bar, then call to be pulled out. Soon Hoeke found a body in the tunnel. It was a small boy. Hoeke felt the limp wrist and found a pulse.

"I've found someone," he called back. "And he is still alive!"

Carefully he dug and dug until he could pull the boy free. Then he called back into the lobby.

"I've got him. Pull me out. But do it slowly."

The other fireman grabbed Hoeke's heels and pulled him gently backward. Carefully the man and the boy were dragged out into the lobby. Within a few minutes, the sobbing boy was telling his story. He had been sitting behind the box seats, in the first row of the balcony, he said, when he heard a woman sitting behind him scream. Then the roof had fallen in, and the balcony had given way. His friend, he told them, was still buried in there somewhere.

From where the firemen stood they could tell that not all of the balcony had collapsed. The Chief turned to the fireman nearest him.

"You," he said, pointing to Bill Hoeke and his friend. "Tell the Ladder Company men to pop the doors off in the back of the building. See if you can get into the auditorium that way. If you can, check the balcony and see if anyone is still up there."

The firemen quickly did as they were told. They found the doors in back of the stage unblocked and easily made their way into the theater. In the auditorium, they found a pile of rubble higher than a man's head. They shone their lights up toward the ragged edge of what had been the balcony to see if anyone was there.

"Hey, down there!" a man's voice called from the darkness. "Up here! On the balcony!"

In the dim light the firemen could see four people. They were sitting calmly on top of the collapsed ceiling with the snow falling all around them through the hole in the roof.

"Are you all right?" Hoeke called.

"We're okay," Dick Richardson answered. "My wife and I have a few cuts and bruises. The backs of the seats kept most of the ceiling off of us. Can you get us down?"

The firemen quickly found a long pole, which they leaned against the shattered edge of the balcony. Bob Richardson quickly wrapped her legs around the pole and slid down. Her husband and the other couple soon joined her on the smashed cement.

"Engine Company 21! Ladder Company 9!" someone was calling as the little group of survivors made its way from the building. "Hurry it up, men! We've got another call."

Hoeke and the other men of Engine Company 21 hurried to their trucks. It was 11:25 and the snow was still falling in the dark night.

"We have a call from Box 245," the men were told. "An apartment house fire."

"Hey, here come the Marines!"

As the three fire trucks rounded the corner, a detachment of Marines marched double time up the street. The men were sweating in the cold air after a two-hour forced march through the knee-deep snow. A mile or so behind them, crews from docked Navy ships were riding in electric trucks that could get through the snow almost as easily as a man could. Behind them, at Fort Meyers, ambulances were being hitched to teams of horses.

It was dawn before the men of Engine Company 21 got back to the Knickerbocker Theater. They had fought three different fires in the past eight hours. Every man was dead tired, but no one suggested that they should go back to the firehouse. Throughout the long night they had thought about the people trapped in the theater.

"I sure hope those Navy boys know what to do," someone said. "There's nothing in our manual about how to lift 10 tons of cement off someone!"

The military personnel sent to the disaster scene did know what to do. Word was quickly sent back to the Navy Gun Works. Soon teams of mules pulling heavy wagons were on the streets of Washington. On the carts were huge hydraulic jacks, which were used in the Gun Works to lift and support large gun barrels.

Once these jacks were in place, the edges of the cement blocks were slowly and carefully lifted upward. With a few inches of extra space in which to work, men could now safely slide under the cement and dig for the trapped people. Some, like the Richardsons, were found with only minor injuries. But more than half of the people in the theater were either dead or dying.

The rescue work continued all through the next day and far into the following night. The injured were taken to nearby homes. The dead were taken to a church a half a block away. The final death toll was close to 100 people.

No one ever knew exactly why the roof of the new theater collapsed. The snow was very wet and more than two feet of it had fallen on the roof. But even this tremendous weight should not have been enough to cause the disaster. It was suggested that the curved wall of the building, on the Columbia Road side, had given way enough to let the roof fall. It was also suggested that the steady vibration of the huge inter-urban cars crossing at the intersection had weakened the building.

What happened to those people who met briefly in the ruins of the theater? The Richardsons moved to Florida, just in time to be caught in the terrible hurricane of 1926. Bob Richardson remembers sitting on her kitchen table, with sea water sloshing all around her, and thinking that another roof was going to fall on her. But this time, her story was different. The roof blew away, along with many of her belongings.

Bill Hoeke stayed with the fire department and eventually became a Fire Commissioner in Montgomery County, Maryland, a suburb of Washington. He answered many calls for help during his long career, but he still feels that the terrible night at the Knickerbocker Theater was the worst.

For 53 years Bill Hoeke didn't know the name of the woman he had rescued from the balcony of the theater. And Boukje "Bob" Richardson didn't know who her rescuer was. Then, in 1975, the two met again, quite by accident, less than 200 miles away from the site of their common adventure. You can imagine the time they had comparing notes on the tragedy at the Knickerbocker Theater.

TRAGEDY AT DONNER PASS

As THEY RODE ALONG, they looked in fear at the mountains ahead. Although it was only the last week in October, snow was already falling. Winter was beginning almost a month earlier than usual. All the trails were covered with snow. Their only guide was the mountain tops, which it seemed they would never reach.

Twelve-year-old Virginia Reed could hardly remember that warm, sunny April day when she and her family had left Springfield, Illinois. At first the trip had been exciting. Just think—going all the way to California by wagon train!

The Reed family had started out with three wagons, each pulled by three yoke, or pairs, of oxen. The big family wagon had been especially built for the long trip. It was a two-story wagon which became known as the *Pioneer Palace Car*. The door to the wagon was on the side, like an old-fashioned stagecoach. Just inside the door was a small room. On either side of the room were spring seats with comfortable high backs. In the center of the little room was a small, sheet-iron stove. A circle of tin in the wagon's canvas cover kept the hot stove pipe from setting the wagon on fire.

Besides Virginia, there was her father and mother, and Patty, age 8, James, Junior, age 5 and Thomas, age 3. Also in the Reed party was Grandmother Keyes, a hired girl and her brother, plus three young men hired to drive the oxen. The Reeds were traveling with the two Donner families from Springfield and planned to join others when they reached Independence, Missouri.

The trip to Independence was a big adventure for Virginia and the other children. Virginia had been allowed to bring her pony, Billy. Part of the time she rode up ahead of the wagon train, one of the first to see what might be over the next hill. At other times she would ride along behind and help herd the cattle that the Reeds and the Donners were taking along to California.

Everything went well until they were part of the way across Kansas. Grandma Keyes was in good health, and the farther west they went, the more her spirits improved. Then they came to the Big Blue River. They found it swollen by the spring rains, and there was no way across except on rafts which had to be built. As soon as the wagons stopped moving, Grandma Keyes's health began to fail. On May 29, 1846, she died.

After crossing the Big Blue River by raft, the wagons pushed on westward. They numbered about forty now, counting those wagons that joined the Reeds and the Donners in Independence. On a good day they made from 15 to 20 miles, shortening or lengthening the distance in order to obtain a good campsite for the night.

An early drawing of the Donner Party showing the Pioneer Palace car.

After several weeks they reached a place called Hasting's Cut-off. This was the beginning of a new trail that passed around the south end of the Great Salt Lake in Utah. According to Lansford Hastings, the explorer who had opened up the route, it shortened the distance to California by 300 miles, and the only bad part was the 40-mile stretch through the desert by the shore of the lake.

There was great debate about which route to take. Finally on July 31, 87 people, including the Reeds and the Donners, left the main party. They set off in high spirits on the Hasting's Cut-off.

A few days travel showed them that the new route was not as good as it had been described. Following the route Hastings had laid out, they soon came to rugged mountains which the wagons could not cross. A new route over the mountains had to be found and progress was slow. As it turned out, it took them a month, instead of the week they had planned on, to reach the Great Salt Lake.

Then there was the long trip across the desert. Hastings said it was only 40 miles. It turned out to be more than 80 miles. In crossing the desert, the Reeds lost most of their cattle and oxen when the animals wandered off in search of water. This meant packing all of their belongings into their smallest wagon and leaving everything else behind.

Upon reaching the western edge of the desert, an inventory of food and other supplies was made. It was clear that the party did not have enough food to last them until they reached California. And to make matters worse, the first storm of the ap-

proaching winter struck the weary travelers. Nearby hilltops were white with snow, and suddenly California seemed far, far away.

It was decided that someone must go ahead to Sutter's Fort on the other side of the Sierra Nevada Mountains and bring back provisions. William McCutchen and C. T. Stanton volunteered. They left in mid-September, carrying letters to Captain Sutter asking for help.

The Reed family and the others pushed on with broken spirits. Both people and animals were exhausted from the five months of hard travel. And disaster was soon to strike again.

Virginia's father got into an argument with John Snyder, one of the drivers, about the best way to handle the oxen. Tempers flared and heated words were exchanged. A fight broke out and Snyder struck Reed several times with his whip. Reed was stunned and partially blinded by the blood streaming from the gashes in his head.

The Donner Party pauses to rest.

When Mrs. Reed saw what was happening, she ran between the two men. But Snyder could not stop—the whip had already started its downward action. Reed's knife was out of its sheath before the first blow struck his wife. He jumped at Snyder. The knife found its target. Snyder fell, fatally wounded.

Snyder was buried the next day and a council meeting followed. The council refused to accept Reed's pleas of self-defense and ordered that he be sent into the wilderness. At first he refused to go. However, his wife pleaded with him to go, since she feared he might meet with violence if he stayed. She also suggested that, if he went on, he could return later and meet them with food.

Reed finally consented to go when the rest of the party agreed to take care of his wife and four children. It was a sad day when James Reed said good-bye and set out alone on horseback. Little did the Reed family realize that this misfortune would later save their lives.

The party traveled on, but there was little happiness left in the group. However, on October 19, the Reeds and the others had reason to rejoice. Stanton and seven mules loaded with provisions returned from California. For the Reeds, Stanton brought something even better than food—news that James Reed was alive. Stanton had met him not far from Sutter's Fort. Stanton had given him a fresh horse and some food. By now he should be at Sutter's Fort organizing a relief party to bring aid to his family and the others.

Stanton helped the Reeds pack what little they had left on one of the mules, and they started out once more. Mrs. Reed, with Tommy in her lap, rode on one mule. Patty and Jimmy rode behind the two Indian guides that returned with Stanton from California. Virginia stayed with Mr. Stanton, thankful to be riding instead of walking as many of the others had to do.

Now, as they traveled westward, winter started in earnest. It was snowing harder, and as the snow got deeper, it became impossible for the oxen to pull the heavy wagons. What provisions they had left were unloaded from the wagons and packed on the backs of the oxen. Another start was made, with men and women walking in snow up to their waists. Some carried children in their arms; others tried to drive their cattle through the snow.

A halt was called when the Indian guides could no longer find the trail. Stanton and the guides went ahead to see if they could find the road. They came back to report that the party could make it now, but they must waste no time in getting over the summit just ahead. Most in the party were so exhausted that they refused to take another step. Those that favored a forced march to the other side of the mountain gave in. Camp was set up within three miles of the summit.

That night it snowed again. Great feathery flakes came whirling down. The air was so full of snow that only objects a few feet away could be seen in the light from the campfire. In the morning the snow lay deep on the mountains.

The group the Reeds were traveling with turned back. They sought temporary shelter during the first days of November in a cabin that had been built by another party trapped by snow two years earlier. Trees were cut down, and two more double-cabins were built. The old cabin became known as the *Breen Cabin,* since it was occupied mainly by the Breen family. The new ones were named the *Murphy Cabin* and the *Reed-Graves Cabin.*

The three cabins were located near a lake, which has since become known as *Donner Lake.* The Donner families had been traveling a few miles apart from the rest of the party for several weeks. They were now camped in Alder Creek Valley below the lake. The snow had come on so suddenly there that they had no time to build cabins. Instead they had hastily put up brush sheds, covering them with pine boughs. In many ways they were worse off than those camped up by the lake.

Most of the cattle were killed for food, and the meat was placed in the snow to keep it from spoiling. Mrs. Reed had no cattle to kill, but she promised the others two cows when they reached California for each one they would give her family now. The hides from the animals were stretched across the cabin roofs to keep most of the snow from drifting in.

At first the time went by rapidly. As soon as the storm let up, there was work to be done. Firewood had to be cut; the cabins had to be made more weatherproof; food had to be brought in, and doz-

The Donner Party on the way to the summit.

ens of other tasks needed to be taken care of. And plans had to be made on how they could get over the mountain before it was too late.

It was decided the only solution was for some of the strongest to try to escape across the mountain pass. This would leave more food for those that stayed behind. On November 12, the first clear day, 15 adults decided to try to cross the mountain. They made it over what was to become known as *Donner Pass* and spent the night camped just beyond. However, afraid that they couldn't make it, they returned to the cabins by Donner Lake on the second day.

A second attempt was made on November 21. However, the snow was so deep the group was forced to return before the day was over.

More snowstorms followed. Some lasted for several days. Others were periods of stormy weather lasting only a few hours or a day at the most. Patrick Breen recorded in his diary that by December 13, the snow was eight feet deep on the level ground.

On December 16, just nine days before Christmas, a group of 17 started out on a third attempt to escape. Two gave up and returned to camp the first day. The others, ten men and five women, kept on going. They carried only enough food to last them six days. It took them two days to get across the top of the pass.

They kept on going because it seemed useless to turn back. Later they were called the *Forlorn Hope* party. According to the dictionary, this name describes a group selected, usually from volunteers, to perform an almost hopeless undertaking. In this case the name certainly was appropriate.

By the ninth day the group ran out of food. A storm kept them huddled beneath a few thin blankets for the next two days and two nights. Four of them died. A fifth member had been left behind on the trail before the storm struck. The others could survive only by turning to cannibalism. Half frozen and starved beyond belief, the ten survivors ate their dead friends in one last effort to escape death.

Then they struggled on—cold, exhausted and weak from starvation. As they came down off the mountains to where the snow lay only in patches, they were lucky enough to kill a deer. But the food was too late, and three more of the party died. The remaining seven, two men and five women, struggled on until they came to a village of friendly Indians. From there they were taken to a ranch in the Sacramento Valley where they were nursed back to health.

While the Forlorn Hope party was battling its way across the snowy mountains, Christmas came and passed at the cabins on Donner Lake. Virginia could hardly remember what Christmas had been like a year ago in Illinois. It seemed so long ago and so much had happened since. She had even more trouble imagining what Christmas would be like next year. Would they all be together in warm and sunny California? She didn't want to think about the other possibilities.

Mrs. Reed had decided weeks earlier that her children would have a treat on the special day. She had laid away a few dried apples, some beans and a small piece of bacon. When the children saw what she had for them, they jumped up and down with joy. The food was cooked carefully so not a scrap would be wasted. When they sat down to eat, Mrs. Reed said, "Children, eat slowly, for this is one day you can have all you want."

As 1846 ended and the new year began, the situation in the camps got worse. Most of the families had run out of beef. Many were trying to live on the cattle hides. If the hides were boiled long enough, they produced a gluelike soup. It tasted terrible but it gave a little nourishment.

When the food ran low at the Reeds, they killed their dog. Mrs. Reed and her four starving children lived on the dog for a week, eating everything but the bones. There were more deaths, and stories of people in the other cabins eating their dead relatives. Mrs. Reed was determined this would not happen to her family.

Meanwhile, at Sutter's Fort, work was under way to organize a relief party. Captain Sutter offered to do everything possible to help. He gave Reed and another man horses and provisions.

The two started out for the mountains and went as far as possible with the horses. Then they placed the provisions in backpacks and proceeded on foot. However, a storm set in, and they finally were forced to return to Sutter's Fort.

Captain Sutter advised them to go on to Yerba Buena, which is now San Francisco, for help. All of the able-bodied men at Sutter's Fort were in south-

Rescue at last!

ern California fighting in the Mexican War. Reed took his advice and went to the naval officer in charge at Yerba Buena to plead for help.

Reed was at Yerba Buena when the seven members of the Forlorn Hope party arrived from across the mountains. News of their famished condition told the story of what it must be like at Donner Lake. Cattle were killed at once, and the men stayed up all night drying beef and making flour.

A party of seven, under the command of Captain Tucker, left as soon as enough beef and flour had been prepared. They had a long and difficult journey. They finally reached the cabins by the lake on the evening of February 18, 1847.

The cabins were almost completely covered with snow. The rescue party shouted to see if anyone was alive. Mr. Breen climbed up the icy steps from his cabin and shouted back, "Relief, thank God, relief!" His words echoed across the mountains and also were repeated a hundred times or more by the other thankful survivors.

There was food and rejoicing. There was news that other relief parties were being organized to bring them more food and to rescue them. And there was sadness, because several had died just days before the relief party had arrived. Among them was Milt Elliot, a faithful friend, who had seemed like a brother to the Reed children.

On February 22, a party of 23 started out in one more attempt to reach safety. In the party was Mrs. Reed and her four children. It was a bright sunny day. The good weather, plus the food brought by

Captain Tucker four days earlier, had put every-body in good spirits. However, they had not gone far when Patty and Tommy Reed gave out, unable to make their way through the deep snow.

At first Mrs. Reed said she would go back with the children. The leaders of the party didn't think it was a good idea and would not allow her to do so. Finally, Mrs. Reed agreed to let Mr. Glover take the two children back to the Breens' cabin. As they parted, Patty said, "Mother, keep going and maybe you will meet father. And don't worry, I'll take care of Tommy."

The party went on. The men wearing snowshoes broke a path, and the others followed in their tracks. At night they lay down to sleep, only to awaken in the morning to find their clothes frozen. At the break of day they were on the trail again.

They were able to make better time when the snow was frozen. The sunshine, which at first seemed to be such a blessing, only added to their misery. The sun's heat melted the snow's crust and made the going all the more difficult. The heat from the sun melted the frozen clothing, making it cling to their damp bodies. And the dazzling reflection of the bright sun off the snow blinded them.

In spite of the hardships and misery, they kept on going. They expected soon to reach a cache of food. It had been left a few days earlier by Captain Tucker while he was on his way over the mountains to rescue them. When they reached the tree where the food had been hung, they were horrified to find that wild animals had found it first.

Deep freeze on wheels! Streamliner
City of San Francisco *snowbound near*
Donner Pass in 1952.

Fortunately the new threat of starvation did not last long. The next day was the most wonderful day in the memories of the Reed family. At about noon they met Mr. Reed and a rescue party of 14. Mrs. Reed, exhausted, sank to her knees and said a prayer of thanksgiving. Virginia and Jimmy ran to their father. He threw his arms around them and there were hugs and kisses. Reed helped his wife to her feet, and for a long time he held her tightly as they all cried.

When Reed learned that two of his children were still at the cabins, he hurried on. If only he could reach them before they died of starvation. He flew over the snow, covering in two days the distance that it had taken five days for Virginia and the others to travel.

When he arrived at Donner Lake on March 1, he was overjoyed to find Patty and Tommy alive. However, the deathlike look of the famished little children made his heart ache. He made soup for the children and the other suffering survivors. He filled Patty's apron with biscuits. She carried them around, giving one to each person.

Reed organized a party of 17 which he would lead across the mountains. Three of his men were left behind to bring in wood and help those unable to travel. Reed also left behind seven days' provisions—not much, but far more than they had eaten in recent weeks.

Reed's party had not traveled far when a new storm broke upon them. The men worked all the first night trying to erect some crude shelters. For three days and three nights they were exposed to the fury of the hurricane of snow. As the storm continued, they ran out of food. When the storm let up, once again they were on the trail. It was a long hard trip, but they finally reached Sutter's Fort.

At long last the Reed family was all together again. Seated around a roaring fire at Sutter's Fort, Mr. and Mrs. Reed, Virginia, Patty, Jimmy and Tommy ate and made plans for a new life in California. The Reeds, the family who had suffered the most hardship on the first part of the trip, were all safe. They were the only family not to lose one or more members in the tragedy at Donner Pass.

A view of the Donner Pass.

THE SCIENCE OF WINTER STORMS

DURING THE WARM DAYS of summer, the sun stands high in the sky. As the earth moves on its year-long trip around the sun, its tilted axis causes the angle of the sunlight to change. On the first day of autumn (about September 23) the sun hangs over the equator. For the next six months, until the first day of spring, the rays of the sun strike the United States at a sharper angle. Because of this, the sun's heat is spread out more in the winter than it is in the summer.

Perhaps you have seen this idea demonstrated. A flashlight is shone down on a table top. It forms a small, round circle of light. If the flashlight is tipped, the light hits the table top at an angle. It is now spread out over a large area. The spread-out light is not as bright as it was before. The amount of light and heat hitting any one spot is much less.

Of course, this is only part of the explanation of why we have seasons. The way the earth revolves around the sun with its axis tilted results in the Northern Hemisphere having more hours of sunlight in summer than in winter. The longest day occurs on about June 21. From then until around December 21 the days get shorter. The parts of the earth having the fewest hours of sunlight receive less heat energy. As a result, those areas slowly cool off, and winter weather sets in.

For the northern parts of the United States and near the tops of the high mountains, winter storms are a threat from September through May. During the four coldest months of the year (December, January, February, and March) as many as 35 violent winter storms may smash at various parts of the country.

Winter storms may take many forms. They often bring very cold temperatures. Heavy snows may fall. Freezing rain or drizzle can coat everything with a glaze of ice. Sleet and hail often pound the earth. Or all of these may hit us during the same winter storm.

While no two winter storms are exactly the same, they all can cause misery and death. Thousands of square miles of land can be cut off from the rest of the world. Millions of living things, including human beings, will suffer and often die before help can reach them. Even in the warmer areas, where it rarely snows, a sudden drop in temperature can cause the loss of millions of dollars worth of crops.

Even the fate of a country can depend upon winter weather. Several times during the American Revolution, winter storms helped the American Army, and in other battles the weather helped the British. Russia was saved twice by winter storms. Napoleon had to retreat from Moscow after the Russians burned the city in 1812 because he knew he could not survive the winter in the open. In 1943–44, winter storms again came to the aid of the Russians when the Germans tried to capture Moscow and Leningrad.

Most of the storms in the United States move from west to east. Some winter storms start off the coast of Asia and travel across the Pacific. These storms can strike the coast anywhere between Alaska and Southern California.

Most of the moisture in these western storms is dropped along the coast or on the western slopes of the mountains. This is because the damp air is forced upward by the slope. As it rises, the air cools. The cold air cannot hold as much moisture as it did when it was warmer. The extra water falls as rain or snow. These storms can strike without warning. In 1846, a storm, that was probably caused in this way, trapped the Donner wagon train. In 1952 a modern train was caught in the same area by a similar storm. It took three days to rescue the passengers.

A few storms manage to slip over the mountains and reform. Colorado and the Texas and Oklahoma panhandle areas are the breeding grounds for some of our worst storms, such as the Blizzard of '49. These mid-western storms generally move toward the Great Lakes, across the northeast, and then off the coast of New England.

The Great Lakes themselves are often the center for the development of winter storms. Storms that form here also usually follow a track to the east.

The center of most of the big storms that move through the eastern United States take a turn to the

Cold and hunger are some of the hardships endured by people stranded because of heavy snows. Here during the 1800s a team struggles through the snow to obtain provisions.

northeast over the eastern part of the country. When the center of the storm, moving eastward, is off the coast, we usually have what is known as a "nor'easter" to those living along the coast. This storm has strong winds sometimes reaching near-hurricane force from Cape Hatteras, North Carolina, northwards. Such winter storms may leave heavy snows over much of the inland sections, westward toward the mountains. A nor'easter may hit a coastal city without much warning. The famous Hurricane Hunter airplanes of the United States Navy and the Airforce are now flying into these storms in an effort to track them more accurately.

Every winter has its bad storms. The people caught in them do not really care how widespread the storm damage is. They are concerned for themselves, their loved ones and their property. But, for the country as a whole, some winters are much worse than others. On the average, 100 people in the United States will die each winter because of storms. But the Great Blizzard of 1888 killed more

than 400 people. The storms during the winter of 1966 caused the deaths of 354 people. And a total of 345 people died in the winter storms of 1958.

A winter storm does not need to dump tons of snow or ice on us to be dangerous. An unexpected drop in temperature can be as deadly as a snowstorm. Even along the warm coast of the Gulf of Mexico, temperatures of 2°F below zero have been recorded. Temperatures in New England have been as low as 30°F, 40°F and even 50°F below zero! In the western mountains, records of 50°F and 60°F below zero are common. Alaska, of course, holds the record for the lowest temperature ever recorded in the United States with a terrible −76°F.

The Weather Service tries to warn us of a sudden drop in temperature. When you hear the words "cold wave warning" in a weather forecast, you know that you must get ready for temperatures lower than normal.

But you also know that the temperature readings do not tell the whole story of a cold wave. If the wind is blowing against your unprotected face or hands, you have discovered that it feels a lot colder than it really is. Going out into temperatures that are near zero can be dangerous if a brisk wind is blowing.

Scientists who work in the far north country have a chart to help them figure the effects of the wind. They call it *the wind-chill factor chart.*

To read this chart, simply find the temperature on the top line. Then read down the chart until you

WIND CHILL EQUIVALENT TEMPERATURES (°F)

WINDSPEED (MILES PER HOUR)	35	30	25	20	15	10	5	0	−5	−10	−15	−20	−25	−30	−35	−40	−45
CALM	35	30	25	20	15	10	5	0	−5	−10	−15	−20	−25	−30	−35	−40	−45
5	33	27	21	16	12	7	1	−6	−11	−15	−20	−26	−31	−35	−41	−47	−54
10	21	16	9	2	−2	−9	−15	−22	−27	−31	−38	−45	−52	−58	−64	−70	−77
15	16	11	1	−6	−11	−18	−25	−33	−40	−45	−51	−60	−65	−70	−78	−85	−90
20	12	3	−4	−9	−17	−24	−32	−40	−46	−52	−60	−68	−76	−81	−88	−96	−103
25	7	0	−7	−15	−22	−29	−37	−45	−52	−58	−67	−75	−83	−89	−96	−104	−112
30	5	−2	−11	−18	−26	−33	−41	−49	−56	−63	−70	−78	−87	−94	−101	−109	−117
35	3	−4	−13	−20	−27	−35	−43	−52	−60	−67	−72	−83	−90	−98	−105	−113	−123
40	1	−4	−15	−22	−29	−36	−45	−54	−62	−69	−76	−87	−94	−101	−107	−116	−128
45	1	−6	−17	−24	−31	−38	−46	−54	−63	−70	−78	−87	−94	−101	−108	−118	−128
50	0	−7	−17	−24	−31	−38	−47	−56	−63	−70	−79	−88	−96	−103	−110	−120	−128

are opposite the speed of the wind. For example, suppose your thermometer reads +5°F and the wind is blowing at 30 miles per hour. You find the column headed +5 on the top line. You follow that column down to 30 miles per hour wind speed and you read −41°F. The chill-factor of the wind turns a temperature of +5°F into a killing 41°F below zero! A person who is dressed for a +5°F temperature would quickly freeze to death in this storm.

Low temperatures, plus wind, plus snow over a period of time make a blizzard. This is the most dangerous of all winter storms. Many of the storms you read about in this book were blizzards. The Weather Service sends out two kinds of warnings for these types of storms. A simple *blizzard warning* means that you can expect winds of at least 35 miles per hour, temperatures of 20°F or lower, and a lot of snow for several hours. If you hear a *severe bliz-*

Blizzards have been important throughout history. The winter of 1777-1778 was a difficult time for the American troops billeted at Valley Forge. This engraving shows General Washington and Lafayette visiting the cold and hungry men.

zard warning, you should get ready for temperatures of 10°F or lower, winds of 45 miles per hour or more and blinding snow.

Snow is frozen water vapor. It forms high in the air. Here the air is holding all of the moisture it can. The extra water vapor freezes into the large, white, six-sided snowflakes. If the snow falls through a layer of warm air, the flakes may join together and form huge, wet snowflakes.

If you have never been in a blizzard, try to imagine what it must be like. If the temperature is 20°F and the wind is blowing at 35 miles per hour, the chill-factor makes the temperature feel the same as −20°F on a calm day. In a severe blizzard, the air would feel the same as 38°F below zero in still air. Add to these terribly cold temperatures a heavy snow, blowing so thickly that you cannot see more than a few feet in front of you, and you have a blizzard.

Ice storms are another very dangerous kind of winter storm. If the temperature near the ground is below freezing (32°F) and the temperature of the air some distance above the ground is above freezing, you may be in for an ice storm if rain is expected.

Ice storms are caused by warm air. Imagine that it has been very cold and clear for several days. You are in the middle of a mass of cold air. The weather report says that a "warm front" is on the way.

"Good," you think. "Now it will warm up for a while."

But watch out! Before that warm air reaches you, you may have trouble.

Because the warm air is lighter, it rises up and over the cold air. The warm moist layer of air that is on top becomes cooler as it rises. Since the air cannot hold as much water as it could when it was warmer, clouds form. Rain begins to fall. But the temperature near the ground is still very cold. The water freezes as it hits the ground and a glaze begins to form.

Tons of ice may cover every large tree. Ice forms on electric power lines. Sometimes the weight is too great. The tree limbs break. The wires fall. Thousands of people lose their electric power and telephone service.

However the biggest danger of ice storms is on the ground. The glaze of ice will cover the sidewalks and the roads causing people to slip and fall on the ice, sometimes receiving serious injuries. Automobile accidents are common. Most of the people who die during ice storms are killed in traffic accidents.

Sleet usually accompanies ice storms. In an ice storm, the water falls as a liquid and freezes before it hits the ground. Sleet is frozen rain. Sleet hits the ground in solid form. You can tell sleet from rain because the sleet will bounce when it hits something. Sleet will not stick to wires or tree limbs. But if enough sleet collects on the ground, driving and walking can become dangerous.

In the high, steep mountains of the world, another winter danger is the avalanche. The word "avalanche" can be used to mean any type of material sliding or falling down the side of a mountain. In this book, you have read about avalanches of snow and ice.

Scientists can identify dozens of different types of snow or ice slides. There are, however, only two main types. One of these is the *slab avalanche*. A mass of snow or ice breaks loose from the mountain peak and slides down the slope. In this type of avalanche, the sliding material is tightly packed together. It changes its course when it strikes something, or it climbs up and over the object blocking it.

The second type of avalanche is often called a *dust avalanche*. In these slides, the snow is not tightly packed. Instead, it is loose and fluffy. This condi-tion usually happens in the dead of winter, when the temperature of the air is very cold. The droplets of snow trap air as they move down the slope until the avalanche is formed by a huge cloud. The air in the valley is forced out of the way of the rushing cloud, which may be traveling at more than 200 miles an hour. People, houses, even trees may be knocked over by the wind hundreds of feet in front of the avalanche.

The main cause of avalanches is too much snow falling on a steep slope. But the scientists who study avalanches have found that the problem is much more complicated than this. How heavy the snow is, how well the snow crystals will hold together and how slippery the base of the snow bank is are all important questions. The strength and direction of

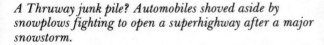

A Thruway junk pile? Automobiles shoved aside by snowplows fighting to open a superhighway after a major snowstorm.

the wind, the temperature and the amount of trees and undergrowth also control whether or not an avalanche will start.

Once the snow is balanced on the side of a high mountain, almost anything can start it down the slope. Even the sound of thunder, a gun shot or a passing airplane can be dangerous. It is often possible to trigger an avalanche before the snow builds up to a dangerous level. Often loud noises are used to do this. Skiers may cross a slope at just the right point and cause a small, not-too-dangerous slide to begin. Sometimes it may be necessary to fire a round of artillery into a mass of snow to get it to move.

Armies fighting in the Alps during World War I learned how to use avalanches as weapons. More than 10,000 Austrian and Italian troops were killed by avalanches on one day in 1916. During this war, at least 60,000 people were killed by slides, many of them started by enemy troops.

Engineers are experimenting with various types of anti-avalanche structures. Metal and stone embankments have been built across the paths of some of the largest avalanches in the hope that these will change the course of the slide or even stop it. Other structures have been built near the tops of some mountains in an attempt to stop the build-up of the snow there.

Several hundred people are killed by avalanches each year in spite of modern warning systems and better anti-avalanche buildings. Quite often a person buried by an avalanche will die very quickly. Slab avalanches usually crush their victims. People caught in dust avalanches generally smother to death in the powdery snow. But many times, a person buried in an avalanche is lucky and stays alive until he can be rescued.

The fastest way to find a person buried in the snow is with an avalanche dog. These animals, usually Alsatians or Belgian Shepherds, have been trained to use their sense of smell to find avalanche victims.

Winter storms of all kinds are dangerous. Traffic accidents and heart attacks are about equally deadly during winter storms. A few people freeze to death in some storms. Others are killed in fires caused by overloaded heating systems. Still more die in stalled cars, killed by the carbon monoxide gas produced by motors kept running to keep the people warm. Falls on the ice kill some people each year. Electric wires downed by ice are also dangerous. And, occasionally, a building will collapse because of the weight of snow and ice, trapping and killing the people inside.

Usually it is difficult to get out of the way of a bad winter storm. In most cases we must simply wait until the weather clears and the temperature goes back to normal. There are many things a person can do to make "riding out the storm" easier and safer. The most important is to listen to the warnings and advice of the Weather Service. It is difficult to predict exactly how bad a winter storm will be, but many people die each year because they did not listen to the directions of the weather scientists.

In order to keep up with the latest weather information, you will need a portable radio or television set. Remember that bad storms quite often destroy electric power lines. Your home may be without electricity for several hours or days.

Of course, you will need a supply of food that will last through the storm. But without electricity, it might be impossible to cook your food. So, for such an emergency, the food should be the kind that can be eaten without cooking. Or you could have an emergency source of heat for cooking.

Staying warm during a winter storm is a serious problem. Homes that are heated electrically can lose their source of heat easily. Most central furnaces that burn fuel oil or gas depend upon electricity to operate the fan that blows the hot air through the house. Many people forget that these furnaces will not work if there is a power failure. However, if you dress warmly and stay indoors, you have a good chance of surviving, even if your house is cold.

Staying indoors during a winter storm is very important. Many people get lost only a few feet from their homes during blizzards. Shoveling snow, pushing cars, even just walking through heavy snow is terribly hard work. Becoming overly tired can bring on heart attacks in anyone who is not in perfect physical condition.

Many of the same rules apply to people who are traveling by automobile during the winter months. The most important rule is to listen to the weather warnings constantly. In many parts of the country, a winter storm can strike quickly.

People traveling by car during the winter should always carry certain emergency supplies. The chance of being trapped for several days is always there. Before starting out on such a trip, the car should be as well prepared as possible. It should have a full tank of gas. It should be in good mechanical condition. Its heater should work well. It should have snow tires, and a set of chains should be carried. Also in the trunk should be a supply of food, blankets or sleeping bags, a shovel, a sack of sand, a camping heater, tow chains and a fire extinguisher.

If you are trapped in a car, your best bet is to stay where you are. Remember the chill-factor. If you stay out of the wind, you will be warmer and less likely to freeze to death than you would be out in the open. It is easy to get lost in blowing snow. And it is easier for rescue parties to find a car on the side of the highway than it is to find a person alone in the woods or fields.

By staying in your car you will also avoid over-exertion. Do not spend too much effort trying to dig your car from the snow bank. The danger of heart attack is always a threat to the person who is working in the cold.

In spite of the cold, a window must be left open in a trapped car. Wet snow can make a car air tight causing the people inside to suffocate. If you must run the motor of the car to keep the heater going, you face the danger of dying of carbon monoxide poisoning. Therefore, ventilation is always necessary.

Keep awake as much as possible, and exercise regularly. Clapping hands and moving your legs are necessary when you are in a cramped car for a long time. Someone should always be awake, to watch for signs of carbon monoxide poisoning in the other people and to be ready to signal to rescue crews. As soon as the storm lets up a little, people will be searching the highways. But a car buried in a snowbank along the side of the road may be overlooked.

Winter storms can cause great hardships. But what kind of a world would it be if there were no winter storms? Without the moisture of the heavy winter snows, the *breadbasket of America,* where much of our wheat, corn and other crops are grown, would become a barren desert. The number of insects is controlled by winter temperatures, and a mild winter is often followed by a larger number of insects in the summer. No snow would mean no skiing—no recreation for thousands and no income for those in the tourist business. How many other ways can you think of that your life would be different without winter storms?

EARTHQUAKES

SAN FRANCISCO 1906

POLICE SERGEANT JESSE COOK looked at his watch. It was 12 minutes after five o'clock. His beat was the fruit and vegetable market of San Francisco and it was busy this time of morning. Nearby farmers had brought their produce by horse-drawn wagons and were getting their goods ready to sell to early shoppers.

As he stood on the corner of Washington and Davis Streets, chatting with a friend, Sergeant Cook noticed the sudden restlessness of the horses. It was followed immediately by a deep rumbling sound that seemed to come out of the earth. He looked up Washington Street and saw the brick surface of the street rippling. He later remembered, "It was as if the waves of the ocean were coming toward me, and billowing as they came."

In another part of town, newspaper editor John Barrett and some of his co-workers had just finished work. They were standing on the sidewalk waiting for an early morning trolley car. Suddenly they found themselves staggering as the earth beneath their feet moved rapidly. The next thing they knew, they were lying on the ground. They tried to get up but couldn't. Barrett saw the buildings around him sway and the trolley tracks twist in the street. Electric wires broke and were "wriggling like serpents, flashing blue sparks all the time." There were gashes in the streets and water from broken pipes sprayed like giant fountains into the air. They noticed the smell of leaking gas.

The first low, growling, unseen rumble changed to a roar made up of the jangling of broken glass, the grinding of stone against stone, and the splintering of wooden buildings.

On a hill overlooking San Francisco, a surprised Bailey Millard sat amid his scattered easel, canvas, paints, and brushes. He had started the day trying to capture on canvas the way San Francisco looked when the sun first touched its buildings.

He watched buildings collapse in the city below. Seven million dollars' worth of stone and bricks was shaken off of City Hall. Its framework remained standing, like the bones of an upright skeleton.

All of this happened in only 65 to 75 seconds. It seemed like an eternity to those who felt it.

People all over town were rudely awakened. Many ran out into the streets in their night clothes, or less, when they realized what was happening. Some were pinned beneath the wreckage of their houses and were rescued later. Others were killed by falling beams and bricks. Everywhere, people were dazed and confused.

San Francisco had suffered other earthquakes. But most of them had been only slightly felt, if at all. Almost 100 years before, in 1808, an earthquake was reported in the area but there weren't many people to feel it. There was a large one in 1836, and another in 1838.

In 1848 gold was discovered in California and people rushed to that sparsely settled part of the country in hopes of finding riches. San Francisco soon became a booming city with buildings being thrown together hastily to house the newcomers. The population grew from 2,000 to 20,000 in just one year. By 1900 there were more than 340,000, and two years later it was estimated there were 485,000 people living there.

Minor earthquakes were felt regularly and were mostly ignored. There were larger ones that caused damage to buildings, but rarely was anyone killed. The big killer was fire.

The combination of flimsy wooden buildings and the stiff breezes that whipped around San Francisco's hills made uncontrollable fires difficult to prevent. Fire fighters and fire fighting equipment became important to the city. And soon builders were paying more attention to whether or not building materials were fireproof.

The sumptuous Palace Hotel was built to withstand both fire and earthquake. Its foundation rested on cement pillars that were buried 12 feet into the ground. Its two-foot-thick brick walls were strengthened by 3,000 tons of reinforced iron strips. Surely no earthquake could damage such a building.

To guard against fire, there were water storage

One tall house in San Francisco leans on a neighbor that seems not to have been affected by the 1906 quake.

tanks on the hotel roof and in the basement. Even if the city water supply should fail, the Palace would have its own water. In addition to its regular pipes for bathrooms and kitchens, there were five *miles* of water pipe to carry water for fire fighting. There were 350 faucets that were connected to 20,000 feet of fire hose. In each of the 800 hotel rooms there was a heat-sensitive instrument that would automatically sound a fire alarm if the room became too hot. And as if that were not enough, every floor was checked every half hour by watchmen who had to push buttons along the way to signal that everything was all right. If one failed to push any button, the office would assume something was wrong.

The Palace had several fires in the 31 years before the 1906 earthquake, but all were brought quickly under control. The building was considered to be fireproof and earthquake-proof.

San Francisco was a very lively city. Many fortunes were made there, and people were anxious to spend their money. The theater flourished and even New York's Metropolitan Opera Company brought performances to this west coast city. The

The San Francisco earthquake was not the first to strike a major coastal city. This engraving shows Lisbon, Portugal, in 1755 being swept away by a tsunami or sea wave, probably caused by an underwater earthquake. In San Francisco it was fire not water that caused much of the damage.

night before the big earthquake, a world-famous singer performed for the people of San Francisco. The singer's name was Enrico Caruso. He was from Italy.

Just the week before, the papers were full of the news of the eruption of Mt. Vesuvius, in Caruso's homeland. It was said that lava ran in rivers down the mountainside and burned villages as it went. The generous people of San Francisco had collected $23,000 to send to the Italians who were left homeless because of the disaster. The reporters asked Caruso why people kept rebuilding villages around the mountain which erupted regularly. He had no answer.

When the jolts from the earthquake awakened Caruso on the morning of April 18, he was afraid it might have damaged his voice. So he ran to the window, opened it, and sounded a magnificent note to the startled people who had run into the street below. He was badly frightened by the earthquake and vowed never to return to San Francisco. He kept that promise.

Nearly 50 fires were reported in downtown San Francisco before 5:30 that morning. Some were caused by fire thrown into the room from a fireplace. Others were from cooking stoves that were knocked over by the shocks. One that was particularly disastrous was caused when someone lit a fire to cook breakfast. The stove was connected to a chimney that had been blocked by the earthquake, and sparks caused the wall to catch fire. This "Ham and Eggs Fire," as it came to be called, was responsible for the burning of a large section of San Francisco.

All of these fires could probably have been controlled, but the water mains that brought water to the city were broken. Firemen who connected their hoses to fire hydrants found only a small trickle of water which quickly dwindled to nothing. They tried other hydrants, but with the same results. How could they fight fire without water?

In the Italian section of town, many people broke open vats of homemade wine and vinegar to pour on the flames. A few people had water storage tanks on their roofs. When the fire raged out of control and threatened the whole city, the firemen decided to level an area between the fire and the rest of the city with dynamite. But none of this worked. The fires continued to burn.

People whose homes had been damaged only slightly by the earthquake saw them go up in flames. The parks were full of people with no homes and only a few belongings that they were able to carry. Families became separated. For days children and parents wandered through the city looking for each other.

Widow Hazel Yardley had slipped out of the house at five o'clock the morning of the earthquake. She was headed for the produce market when the quake threw her to the ground. When she was able to get up she ran in panic back home, where she had left her two-year-old Annie sleeping.

The house was completely demolished. The woman dug hysterically through the ruins but she couldn't find Annie. Neighbors told her no one could have lived through such destruction, and they led her away from the rubble. She had found a small picture of Annie that she clutched to her.

Hazel Yardley refused to believe that Annie was dead. She wandered through the streets, stopping everyone she saw. Had they seen the little girl in the picture? Always, the answer was the same, "No."

Two days later a policeman took the woman to the Ferry Building and she was put on a boat for Oakland, across the bay. Many children who were alone had been sent across the bay. She searched the face of each child she saw. Every adult was shown the picture. But there was no word of Annie.

By this time Oakland had received 50,000 people who had no homes. There were refugee camps set up for them in various parts of town. Mrs. Yardley steadfastly walked through one camp after another, still searching.

It was after dark when she reached the camp of tents where Harry Adams and his family were sheltered. Adams and his wife were sitting outside their tent, breaking bread into a pot of stew. Mrs. Yardley went up to them and showed her picture and asked her question again.

Mr. Adams got up and went into the tent. He returned with Annie in his arms.

He had rescued her when the house collapsed.

These tracks in San Francisco buckled during the 1906 quake.

Seeing no parent around, he took her with his wife and their two children to safety.

A joyous Mrs. Yardley knelt and gave thanks to God as she hugged Annie to her.

Telephone communications from San Francisco to the outside world were cut off by the earthquake. Telegraph lines went with the fire. The rest of the world was left to guess about the fate of San Francisco, and wild rumors spread about how many had been killed. People living in New York, Chicago, London, Paris, Berlin, and Tokyo read about the raging fire (which was true), about soldiers killing people who were suspected of stealing (which was partly true), and about people dying of starvation (which was not true).

People left the city by ferryboat and by train. The Southern Pacific railroad moved 70 passengers out of the city every minute, eventually taking 300,000 people away from San Francisco. There was no charge for this train trip. The railroad company also shipped into the city 37,000 tons of relief supplies.

The Army, commanded by Brigadier General Frederick Funston, moved in immediately to help keep order. General Funston gave orders that were backed by the mayor to shoot anyone caught stealing. This practice was later severely criticized by the public, and it is difficult now to know how many people were actually killed this way. The general claimed only three cases were reported to him. But there were reports of dozens who were shot. The stories were exaggerated, but no one knows how much.

The Marines and Navy arrived on Thursday, a little more than 24 hours after the earthquake. The fires were still raging. They docked fireboats, hospital boats, and boats carrying fresh water and supplies at the city's piers. They brought more explosives to use in blasting a clear path between the blazing fire and what was left of the city.

For the next 48 hours the fire fighting continued. Several times fires in one section of town would seem to be under control but a fresh wind would whip the embers into flames and leap across dynamited paths to devour another section of town. Firemen worked until they dropped from exhaustion. When one fell, a volunteer would take his place. Finally everything except the waterfront area was under control.

Fire teams concentrated their efforts on that part of town. Inch by inch they gained ground and eventually, on Saturday morning, April 21, the fire was over. Three days before, it had all started. Now it began to rain. Exhausted, sleep-hungry, dazed people cheered.

Even before the fire was out, city officials and a group of citizens had formed a committee to see

San Francisco

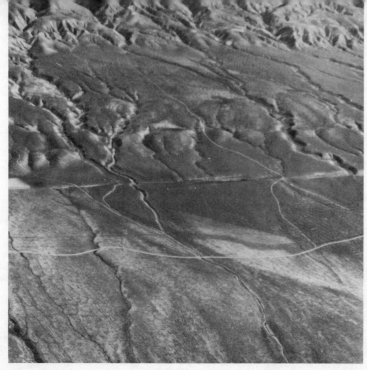

In this aerial view of the San Andreas Fault, the line across the center of the photograph traces a break in the earth's surface. This break lies directly over a section of the earth that is under great strain.

to the needs of the people. Congress had voted emergency funds for food, clothing, medical supplies, and shelter.

In looking over the damaged city, it was discovered that 4.7 square miles of land and 28,000 buildings had burned. This included the Palace Hotel. It was estimated that more than 600 people died from this earthquake. But not all of these people were in San Francisco.

Eighty-seven were patients at Agnews State Insane Asylum near San Jose. Along with them died 11 nurses, the superintendent of the hospital, and his wife. In the city of San Jose, 21 people died. A sawmill at Hinckley Gulch was buried along with nine workers by a landslide.

The earthquake that caused all of this damage left signs along a path that was 200 miles long. This path lies over what is known as the San Andreas Fault. The San Andreas Fault is not just one big crack in the earth down the coast of California. It is a lot of parallel breaks in the surface of the earth—breaks that lie directly over a section of the earth's surface that is under much strain. Scientists think of it as a place where huge pieces of the crust of the earth rub and grind past each other very slowly. Sometimes pressures inside the earth cause these sections to move past each other smoothly and only cause small quakes. At other times these pieces fit together so tightly that they do not move easily. However, the pressure that causes the movement is still there and it builds up. The pressure may even cause the crust to "bend" out of shape a little. When the pressure becomes great enough, the sections will finally move past each other, only now with great force. It has been estimated that the shock waves from this huge build-up of energy in 1906 traveled at two miles-per-second.

At one place along the California coast, where the earthquake traveled under the ocean, its shock was felt by a ship. The *Argo* must have been directly above the fault, because it was as if the ship had been blasted with an explosive. Some of the steel plate of her body buckled. Bolts were blown out of place. Her captain later remembered that for a few seconds, "the whole ship appeared to be breaking up—and in a perfectly calm sea!"

At sea, 150 miles due west of San Francisco, the schooner *John A. Campbell* rose high in the water, hesitated a moment, and then smashed downward again. The sleeping crew jumped from their bunks to see what had happened. When they were on deck, they could see nothing out of the ordinary. It was as if they had all had the same bad dream at once. The captain wrote in the log, "Sudden motion, unexplained. The shock felt as if the vessel struck . . . and then appeared to drag over soft ground." But of course, it could not have dragged soft ground—the ocean bottom was more than 14,000 feet below. It was only later that the captain discovered they had felt the shocks of the earthquake that had ripped up the coast of California.

The shock of the restless movement of the earth's crust plowed a furrow across fields, through barns, over hills, and down stream beds. In many places there were no deaths only because there were no people living there. It demolished whole forests of redwood trees, sent tons of coast-line rocks into the sea, and re-routed the flow of water in creek beds.

All of the effects of the earthquake were not bad. Scientists from the University of California studied the quake and published their findings. This study is thought by some people to be one of the greatest contributions to modern seismology (the study of earthquakes). Up until this time it was generally believed that earthquakes resulted in rocks slipping vertically, leaving one side of a fault higher than the other.

Measurements made along the San Andreas Fault, however, showed that most of the movement was horizontal. Creek beds, roads, and fences that had lain along a straight line now jogged as much as 15 to 20 feet out of line. This idea of horizontal movement was so new that scientists found it hard to believe. In fact, they were hesitant to even discuss it. Those who did, suggested it was a freak occurrence, and not what normally happens. We know today that many faults have more movement in a horizontal direction than they do in a vertical direction.

Earthquakes are measured in two ways. One measure is of the energy that comes from the source of the earthquake. This amount of energy is called the *magnitude* of the quake. Seismographs record information that allows scientists to calculate the magnitude.

The other measurement of an earthquake has to do with how much it is felt and how much damage is done. This is called the *intensity* of an earthquake. Intensity is usually measured by the observations of people who were in the area. These observations are described according to the Modified Mercalli Scale, which is divided into 12 parts, as follows:

I. A shock recorded by seismographs only. Not noticed by people, although they may feel dizzy or nauseated. Sometimes birds and other animals seem uneasy.

II. A shock felt indoors by a few people, especially if they are on the higher floors of a tall building. Hanging objects and tree limbs may sway.

III. This shock is felt by a number of people on lower as well as upper levels of buildings. Automobiles that are standing still may rock slightly.

IV. Many people indoors feel this shock, and a few who are outside. Doors, windows, and dishes may rattle.

V. Almost everyone indoors, even those who were sleeping, may feel this one. Pictures may fall off walls, bells in churches may ring, and furniture may shift slightly.

VI. Everyone, indoors and outdoors, will feel this one. Poorly constructed buildings may be damaged. Furniture may overturn. Windows may break.

VII. People are frightened and run outside. They find it difficult to stand. Drivers of automobiles cannot control the movement of the cars. Well constructed buildings are not damaged, but ordinary buildings suffer some damage. Bricks and stones are dislodged.

VIII. Most chimneys fall. People are alarmed and may panic. Trees shake with some breaking off. Damage to well constructed buildings is slight; ordinary buildings may collapse.

IX. Total destruction of a few buildings. People are generally panic-stricken. There are cracks in the ground. Underground pipes sometimes break.

X. Ground cracks may be several inches wide. Well built wooden buildings and bridges are badly damaged. Cement and asphalt roads may develop open cracks.

XI. Stone buildings are destroyed. Bridges fall, and railway lines are twisted. Pipes buried in the earth are all broken.

XII. Damage is complete. All manmade structures are destroyed. There are great changes in the surface of the earth.

This scale was first set up in 1902 by an Italian seismologist whose name was Mercalli. It was brought up to date in 1931 by two Americans to include such modern things as tall buildings and automobiles. When you use a Mercalli number, it is always written in Roman numerals. It measures intensity, which is determined by people's senses.

The other measurement we mentioned, magnitude, is first taken from a seismograph. This measurement is then adjusted, depending on how far the instrument is from the source of the earthquake.

The strength of the quake is expressed in numbers on a scale called the Richter Scale (after C. F. Richter). Magnitudes usually fall between 3 and 8 (notice, this scale is not written in Roman numerals). However, scientists can measure quakes so small they are felt only by very sensitive instruments. Some are so slight that negative numbers must be used to describe their size.

The 1906 San Francisco earthquake had a magnitude of 8.3. Larger earthquakes have been recorded at 8.8 and 8.9. This is the number you usually read about in newspapers when they describe the size of an earthquake. The story may read, "The magnitude of the earthquake was 4.6 on the Richter Scale." Newspapers often say that the scale runs from 0 to 10, but actually there is no bottom or top to the scale.

There is another thing that is usually not understood about this scale. An earthquake which has a magnitude of 8 is not twice as great as one that has a magnitude of 4. This is because the scale is *logarithmic*. This means that each number on the scale represents 10 times as much energy as the number below it. For instance, magnitude 8 is 10 times greater than magnitude 7. Magnitude 8 is 10×10 (or 100) times greater than magnitude 6. Magnitude 8 is $10 \times 10 \times 10$ (or 1,000) times greater than magnitude 5. And it is a million times larger than magnitude 2 ($10 \times 10 \times 10 \times 10 \times 10$). So instead of magnitude 8 being twice as large as magnitude 4 (as some people mistakenly think), it is really 10,000 ($10 \times 10 \times 10 \times 10$) times as great.

Will there be another disastrous earthquake in San Francisco? Small ones are frequently felt there, and one seismologist has said that, "The further you are from the last big earthquake, the nearer you are to the next."

Just as Caruso could not say why people keep building at the foot of Vesuvius, so we can-

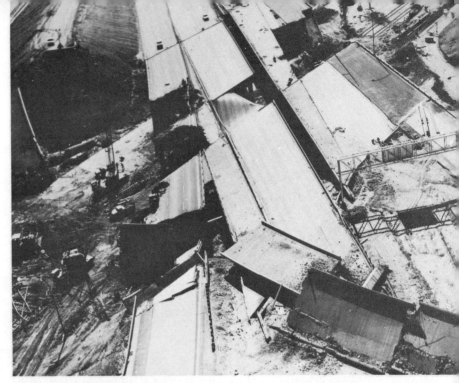

This collapsed highway overpass is a result of an earthquake that shook California.

not explain the rebuilding of San Francisco. It is a beautiful location for a city. Built on seven hills, it sits on a peninsula that has the Pacific Ocean to the west and San Francisco Bay on the east. The sharpness of the hills and the blue of the Pacific endear the place to the people who live there.

In addition, man has a sort of blind faith that he can endure anything that nature can hand out. It is almost like a game to see if he can outwit natural disasters.

And so, whatever the reason, people all over the world continue to rebuild homes that have been destroyed by earthquakes.

ALASKA
MARCH 27, 1964

GOOD FRIDAY, 1964, had been a beautiful day in the part of Alaska that borders on Prince William Sound. The temperature in Anchorage that afternoon reached a point only a few degrees below freezing, and the air was crisp with the gentle fall of powdery snow. At 5:30 in the evening, holiday shoppers crowded the streets. Some thought about the Easter clothes they had bought. Others thought of the eggs to be dyed. Some, perhaps, dreamed of the early spring the warmer weather promised. Surely no one recalled St. Matthew's description of the first Good Friday, "And, behold . . . the earth did quake, and the rocks rent."

But 150 miles to the southeast of Anchorage and 12 miles below the blue waters of Prince William Sound the earth was not as quiet and calm as it seemed on the surface. The rocks lying along an ancient fault had managed to hold together in spite of the pressures that had pushed against them for many years. But these pressures had continued until now the breaking point had been reached. Suddenly, without warning, there were shocks that could be felt on the surface; the rocks along the fault shifted. One side apparently moved upward while the other slipped down. Between 5:36 and 5:41—five short minutes—200,000 megatons of energy were released. This was about

The marquee of the Denali Theater was level with the sidewalk after the ground beneath the theater dropped nearly ten feet during an earthquake.

This sidewalk on 4th Street in Anchorage, Alaska, was broken apart in 1964 by earthquake shocks.

the same amount of energy that would be released if 200 *billion* tons of TNT were to explode all at once. It would take a thousand or more hydrogen bombs to produce this much energy.

At thousands of miles-per-hour, the shock waves rushed toward the surface where half of Alaska's 250,000 people unknowingly waited for disaster. Within these five short minutes 115 of them were to die and 4,500 were to be left homeless. The property damage finally was to total $750,000,000—nearly 100 times what it had cost to buy the entire territory from Russia a century before.

Seismographs all over the world began to record the violent shocks which were to reach 8.5 on the Richter Scale, the highest reading of any earthquake to strike North America in 65 years. But perhaps the first person to "see" the quake was a late shopper in the J. C. Penney store in Anchorage. Admiring several small porcelain figurines, Mrs. Carol Tucker was nearly alone on the third floor of the new, five-story, windowless store. Suddenly, the tiny figures began to dance gently on the glass counter top. Sensing that something was seriously wrong, rather than understanding what was actually happening, Mrs. Tucker walked rapidly toward the escalator. She could feel the entire building shaking, as the dolls had done moments before, and realized that an earthquake had begun. Then, without a warning flicker, the power failed and she was plunged into total darkness.

Now thoroughly frightened, she stumbled along in the dark to the stalled escalator and felt her way as quickly as possible down the shivering metal steps. Heavy objects crashed around her, unseen in the dark. With her arms over her head, she stumbled over the floor that was buckling and weaving as if it were alive. Falling once, badly tearing a ligament in her leg, she finally reached the ground floor. There she could see daylight flowing through the glass display windows that lined the front of the store. With relief, she made her way across the rippling floor to the front door of the store and looked out onto the intersection of 5th Avenue and D Street. There she stopped, watching with shock as a car bounced down the street, its tires sometimes two feet off the ground and its rear fishtailing as its driver desperately tried to control the vehicle. As she stood there, clutching the trembling door frame, the concrete facade of the store broke loose and crashed to the sidewalk in front of her. A man on the sidewalk disappeared under tons of concrete. The bouncing car was hit by one huge slab, fatally injuring its driver. A parked car was later to be dug from the rubble, crushed until it was only 18 inches thick.

A block north, on 4th Street, the shock waves seemed to cut the ground out from under the buildings standing on the north side of the street, leaving the south side untouched. The old Denali Theater dropped nearly ten feet into the ground and finally settled with its nearly undamaged marquee level with the sidewalk.

At the Anchorage International Airport the control tower shuddered with the shock and finally toppled, killing the air traffic controller who was on duty there. The Presbyterian Hospital was left without water, heat, or electricity and patients were treated by doctors and nurses carrying flashlights. Bouquets of Easter flowers were left standing in the lightly falling snow as the florist shop's front crumbled into dust.

Suburban Turn-Again-By-The-Sea was a pleasant residential community of about 300 homes. Many of these stood near the cliff that overlooked Cook Inlet. At the first shock, many of the residents of these houses rushed out to escape the collapsing roofs only to be flung to the ground by sharper jolts. Fissures suddenly opened around them, and then the entire bluff slipped downward toward the churning water below.

But Anchorage was lucky. Although 75 percent of its property was damaged or destroyed, only nine people were killed in that terrible five minutes. But other towns were not so lucky.

About 125 miles due east of Anchorage, at the head of a fiord overlooking Prince William Sound, stands the old gold camp of Valdez. The towering mountains seem to be trying to push the little village into the water, and the steep-roofed houses crowd around the deep-water harbor. Nearly 1,200 people lived here that Good Friday and many of them were at the harbor at 5:36, watching the unloading of the 400-foot steamship *Chena*.

This quaint little town, sometimes called the

"Switzerland of Alaska," was built on loose, silty soil that had been deposited centuries ago by a retreating glacier. A small river flowed across this silt and washed much of it into the fiord. It was on this unstable base that the people of Valdez had built a 100-foot-long pier. The water alongside the pier was deep and the *Chena* was able to unload her cargo directly onto the wooden pier. It was an exciting event to the children of the town and they liked to stand along the sides of the pier in order to see better. This day, being a holiday, and such a beautiful day, many parents also stood on the pier to watch the unloading activities and to chat with each other. Counting the dockworkers who were working the ship, 28 people crowded together near the end of the wooden dock.

No one is exactly certain what happened as the quake's shock waves hit the town. Fissures three feet wide opened up in the soft soil under the town. Houses and buildings collapsed as the loose material upon which they were built shifted. And then, almost immediately, the wave hit the pier.

Some of the people who were on higher ground reported that the water simply rose quickly. Others said that they saw a "wall of water" rush up the fiord. Whatever the case, the sudden onrush of water cut the silt from under the pier. The people who had, moments before, been enjoying their free day, began to run. But before any of them reached the end of the pier, the wooden structure collapsed and all 28 people were

The damage caused by earthquake, fires, and tsunami that struck Alaska in 1964.

Destruction of streets and houses in Turnagain, Alaska, 1964.

caught by the receding water and washed out into the sea.

The people on the island of Kodiak had more warning of the coming wave, since Kodiak is more than 200 miles to the southwest of the earthquake's epicenter. The shock waves were felt all over the island. One man reported that it felt like he "was walking on Jello." The Fleet Weather Station warned of a possible tsunami, and so there was little loss of life.

Some people believe that the animals of Kodiak knew that the earthquake was coming long before humans could feel it. The huge Kodiak bears, for which the island is named, left hibernation two weeks earlier than usual—the day before the quake. Their tracks showed that instead of wandering aimlessly around as you might expect a sleepy bear to do, these bears left their caves and dens on the dead run. Even the domesticated cattle seemed to sense something wrong, and several herds moved high up into the hills earlier than usual.

The first wave was a gradual one, gently flowing in for a while, then gently flowing out. It hit Kodiak at 6:47, more than an hour after the first shock of the earthquake. The quiet, nondestructive first wave warned those people near the beach that the Weather Service warning had been an accurate one.

The second wave was a 30-foot-high wall of water that smashed ashore a few minutes later. It rushed across the harbor, crushing piers and docks, tearing ships loose from their anchors and hurling them into the heart of town. Kraft's General Store is reported to have been lifted from its foundations and floated out to sea, only to float back again on the next wave, then sail back out to sea once more and again be safely returned to shore. Finally it settled on dry land only a few yards from its original foundations.

Down the coast from the town of Kodiak stood the Aleut village of Kagayak. With the first wave, all 41 of the villagers moved to higher ground. After the second wave, a small party of villagers tried to return to their homes to salvage food and other belongings. An hour after the second wave had receded, the third and largest wave crushed the village. Six of the Indians tried to ride out the wave in a small boat. Three were washed overboard.

The third wave did even more damage at Kodiak. The 131-ton crab boat *Selief* was picked up like a cork and dumped ashore. An hour later, the fourth wave floated the boat back into the harbor. Throughout the night, wave followed wave, with only about an hour between each. Dawn on March 28 revealed a ruined island. Only the three Aleuts were dead, but more than half of the fishing fleet was gone or damaged badly, and the canning industry was almost a total loss.

Perhaps it was the little town of Seward, only a few miles west of the epicenter, that received the hardest blow from the Good Friday earthquake. Perched on the upper end of Resurrection Bay,

a short distance from the Gulf of Alaska, Seward and its 1,700 people were important to the economy of the state. Its deep-water port remains free of ice all winter and tons of cargo cross the docks. From here, oil, food, and other necessities for surviving the long winter are shipped inland by rail and by truck.

But the land upon which Seward's waterfront facilities were built was very much like that of Valdez. Streams flowing out of the mountains had washed gravel, sand, and silt into Resurrection Bay. Settling to the bottom, this loose soil formed a steep slope of between 30 and 40 degrees. It was into this uncertain base that the piling of the piers had been driven and upon which many of the warehouses and other buildings of the waterfront had been built. Texaco and Standard Oil Companies had built 16 storage tanks on the same type of soil, and on Good Friday these tanks contained 40,000 barrels of petroleum products.

Nevertheless, the people of Seward were proud of their town. They sponsored an annual salmon fishing competition that had become world famous. They worked hard to blend their city and its industry into the natural beauty of their surroundings. They built parks and libraries and supported their excellent schools. As a result of all this work, Seward had been notified that it had been selected to receive an All American City Award. The ceremony in which this award was scheduled to be presented was to take place one week after Easter.

With the first shocks, nearly a mile of waterfront

slipped into the bay. Docks and piers collapsed as the loose soil under them slid down the steep underwater slope. Undercut by this landslide, all eight of the Standard Oil Company's storage tanks collapsed, pouring thousands of gallons of oil and gasoline into the harbor. At about the same time, the eight Texaco tanks exploded one after another, each with a tremendous roar that drowned out the growling of the earth. Orange flames spread rapidly in all directions as the burning oil ran across the ground and into the sea.

As the first sea wave struck the harbor, the oil-covered water itself burst into flame. Pilings, that had been snapped off by the force of the tsunami, floated upright because their bases were water-logged, and their tops blazed like torches in the water.

No one really knows when the fires finally burned out. Everyone in the ruined town was busy trying to stay alive as wave after wave, six in all, smashed across what had been the four-million-dollar harbor. High school student Linda McRae saw the first wave as it crossed the bay. Quickly, she gathered up her three-week-old nephew and, along with her brother, ran to the back of a neighbor's house. Scrambling in desperation over empty oil barrels, they climbed first onto the roof of a garage and then to the top of the house.

A ship and buoy were washed up across this road in Seward, Alaska, by a tsunami.

Within seconds, the wave hit the garage, breaking it into splinters. Beneath them, the porch of the house washed away, and then parts of the house itself. Finally, the portion of the house to which the three people clung floated free from its foundation and swirled off into the darkness. Linda remembers seeing the raging fire and wondering whether it would eventually reach their bobbing raft.

Battered by floating debris, the remains of the house finally came to rest against four large trees. There the three lucky survivors rode out the rest of the waves and finally, as the water receded, managed to lower themselves into the ruined house.

So far as human deaths were concerned, Seward was fairly lucky. Thirteen of its citizens were killed. Nearby, in the Aleut village called Chenega, the death toll was almost double that of Seward. Chenega had been a cluster of 20 houses, each standing on high pilings. The force of the waves cut these pilings down to the level of the sand and carried off all of the houses. Along with the debris went the bodies of ten adults and 13 children.

It was the property damage in Seward that was so terrible. The docks were gone. The canneries and oil storage areas lay in total ruin. Both the railroad and the highway to Anchorage were cut in dozens of places. The power plant and water treatment plant were both damaged and useless. Cut off, except by air, the citizens of Seward had to take care of themselves as they began to repair the damage of the worst earthquake the United States has suffered in this century.

The full extent of the force of this earthquake was not realized until later. Geologists immediately began a careful survey of the damaged area and discovered that over a million square miles of the earth's surface had been affected in some way.

The earthquake, fires, and tsunami that struck Alaska on Good Friday, 1964, took many lives and caused property damage that finally totalled $750,000,000.

THE TREMBLING EARTH

WE ARE USED TO CHANGES around us. Our friends grow taller and older. The weather and the seasons do not remain the same. Moving water changes the shape of our beaches and river banks. But we like to think that the ground upon which we walk is stable and unchanging.

Each year, however, this "solid" ground trembles, heaves, and cracks hundreds of thousands of times. The best buildings man can build sway and sometimes even crumble while thousands of people die. Cries of "EARTHQUAKE" flash around the world as the earth suddenly changes beneath our feet, leaving us fearful of the unknown.

It is difficult to estimate the damage caused by a major earthquake. The shivering of the ground can be felt over a million square miles of the earth's surface. Loose soil shifts and buildings that are not anchored on solid rock can collapse. The surface of the earth can crack open in huge fissures that often run for miles, cutting through houses, highways, and railroad tracks, tearing them apart. Fissures and the shaking earth can break gas and water lines while uncontrollable fires often add to the damage of the earthquake.

Unstable soil and rocks that happen to be perched on the side of steep hills can shake loose and come crashing down as a landslide, crushing everything below under tons of debris.

But almost as bad as the damage caused directly by the earthquake is the destruction caused by huge sea waves, called *tsunamis*. If the earthquake occurs under the sea, the ocean floor may be suddenly disturbed. This usually causes a series of waves to travel rapidly through the water in all directions, very similar to what happens when you throw a rock into a quiet pond. These tsunamis, however, move across the surface of the ocean at tremendous speeds—sometimes at 500 miles-per-hour. Where the water is deep, the waves are low and commonly pass unnoticed under a large ship at sea. But when the tsunamis enter shallow water, the height of the waves begins to build up. Where the shore is particularly shallow, these waves smash across the beach as a wall of water that can be taller than a ten-story building. So it is possible for an earthquake to kill people and destroy property thousands of miles away within a few hours.

People who live along the edge of the sea near the center of the earthquake's disturbance will have little chance to escape the swiftly moving waves. But, thanks to the Seismic Sea Wave Warning System, warnings of possible tsunamis can be sent out to people living far from the earthquake area. Ten earthquake-recording stations and 20 wave-measuring stations have been built in various parts of the Pacific Ocean. When these instru-

Devastation in Peru.

This is what remained of a building in Messina, Sicily, in 1908 after the shocks of an earthquake traveled through the soft ground.

ments record a quake on the ocean floor and tsunamis spreading out from it, a warning is sent by radio to the governments of those countries likely to be hit. With several hours' notice, it is usually possible to move people away from the beaches. Many lives have been saved by this system.

If an earthquake happens to occur beneath a heavily populated area, the damage to property may be very great. But the most terrible destruction of earthquakes is the number of human lives that is sometimes taken. You have read about some of the most deadly earthquakes in this book. It is often impossible to determine exactly how many people are killed in these catastrophes, particularly if they occurred many years ago, or in countries today whose census figures are inaccurate. Some people estimate that as many as 60,000 people died as a result of the earthquake in Lis-

bon, Portugal in 1755. At least 100,000 people were killed by the quake that destroyed Messina, Italy in 1908. Perhaps 140,000 human beings died in 1923 when an earthquake struck the Kwanto Plain of Japan. And at least 100,000 people were killed in the 1960 catastrophe at Agadir, Morocco. And these terrible stories are only a small sample of the total death toll caused by earthquakes during the history of man. During the last 1,000 years or so there have been at least two dozen earthquakes that have each killed 50,000 or more people.

Earthquakes can and do occur in almost all parts of the world. But they strike most often near the younger mountain ranges of the world. Only a few of the major earthquakes that have occurred during the time man has been writing his history were outside the two great earthquake belts that follow these mountain ranges.

One circles the Pacific Ocean. The other follows the high mountains from Portugal to Burma. Many less dangerous earthquakes occur in the region of the Mid-Atlantic Ridge, a range of mountains that runs down the center of the Atlantic Ocean.

These belts where earthquakes most often occur are almost the same as those in which the most active volcanoes now stand. But we cannot assume that earthquakes are caused by volcanoes. The violent explosion of a volcano may cause the earth to shake and crack, but these "quakes" are very small when compared to a major earthquake.

Geologists, scientists who study the earth, use the word "earthquake" to name what happens when rocks slip suddenly along a crack in the earth. A crack along which the rocks have slipped is called a *fault*. The rocks may move up or down along the fault, or they may move sideways.

On the surface, or deep in the earth where the rocks actually slip along the fault, is a zone called the *focus* of the earthquake. The focus may be confined to a small area, or it may extend for miles along the fault. The focus may be on the surface of the earth and after the earthquake we may be able to see the fault running through the rocks. But most often, the focus of the earthquake is beneath the surface of the earth—generally within about 50 miles of the surface. A few earthquakes, however, will have their focuses several hundreds of miles deep.

If the focus of the earthquake is below the surface of the earth, the waves it produces rush out in all directions. If the earthquake is powerful, these waves may affect the surface of the earth for many miles around. The worst shaking, however, will usually occur on the surface of the earth directly above the focus. This region on the surface, closest to the focus, is called the *epicenter* of the earthquake. It is here that most of the destruction usually takes place.

When the epicenter of an earthquake is near a populated area, scientists and building engineers usually study its effects carefully. They talk to the people who survived to try to find out what they felt; the engineers study buildings and other man-made structures, and they look carefully at the changes that have taken place in the ground.

Using this information, the scientists and engineers can determine the *intensity* of the earthquake. The intensity of an earthquake does not tell us how strong the earthquake was. It only tells us what effects the earthquake had on a certain area. So, intensity is a measure of the power of the earthquake determined from observing man-made structures and the earth's movements or cracks.

These effects, however, do not always tell much about the strength of the earthquake. How deep the focus of the earthquake is will have a lot to do with how extensive the earthquake is. A powerful earthquake whose focus is very, very deep may do less damage than one that is much weaker but whose focus is closer to the surface. For example, the earthquake that destroyed Agadir, Morocco in 1960 and killed 100,000 people was only about 1/100 as strong as the 1923 earthquake in Japan, but its focus was closer to the surface.

The conditions of the surface above the focus—the epicenter—also may cause a weaker earthquake to result in more damage than a stronger one would have elsewhere. A strong quake whose focus is under the ocean or under an uninhabited area may have little effect on a populated area of the earth. Or if the earthquake takes place under a region of solid rock or of tightly packed, dry soil the damage at the epicenter may not be very great. On the other hand, certain types of soil that seem quite solid even when they are wet may turn "soupy" when they are shaken by an earthquake. And the result may be tremendous damage to the buildings constructed on them.

The strength of an earthquake is known as its *magnitude*. Hundreds of *seismograph* instruments around the world constantly wait for the earth to shake. These instruments record the magnitude of each of the million or so quakes that occur each year. These records are quickly sent to thousands of scientists around the world and, with the help of computers, these men and women work together to find the location of each earthquake's epicenter, focus, and magnitude. Within minutes after the earthquake strikes, and often long before the survivors can send out word of the disaster, help and warnings of possible tsunamis may be on their way.

The scientific study of earthquakes has also shown engineers and builders how to construct buildings that can better withstand the shocks of earthquakes. Learning how to do this has not been an easy job, and is not yet complete. Scientists and engineers from almost every country in the world are now working together to solve this important problem.

It is fairly easy to build a building that must simply hold up under its own weight and the weight of its contents. These weights are pulled straight down by gravity and can be measured easily. And

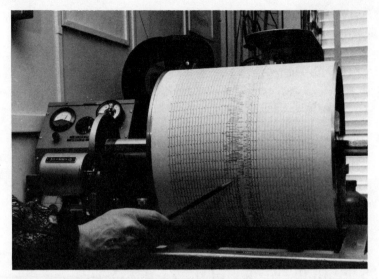

This seismographic recording indicates earthquake tremors or shocks. Note the variation in the waves.

it is fairly easy to experiment on various building materials to determine how much downward pressure they can stand before they break.

But a building in an earthquake must withstand forces pushing it in all directions. Sometimes the ground moves upward under a building. Often the ground moves back and forth or twists the building's foundations. The builder must tie all parts of the building together carefully to withstand any possible force moving in almost any direction. And, because it is so difficult for him to experiment with these forces in a laboratory, the builder must often wait for an earthquake to strike his building before he can learn whether or not he has made a mistake.

Many scientists are trying to make instruments that will predict the coming of an earthquake. They know that the pressures that cause the rocks to slip along the fault slowly build up over a period of time. Sooner or later the pressure will become too great and the rocks will break loose suddenly and violently. So far, these studies have not been very successful. However, scientists in both Japan and the United States are working together on this problem and are making progress. Someday, perhaps within the next few years, we will be able to predict when a large earthquake will occur far enough in advance to save many lives.

Other experiments are being tried that may prevent serious earthquakes entirely by causing small, less dangerous ones. In the western part of the United States, scientists are using water to cause small rock slippages—a little at a time—along faults, thus hoping to avoid one large slip, or quake. To do this, holes are drilled into the face of the fault. Measured quantities of water are then pumped into the crack between the rocks. The water makes the fault face slippery and adds weight to the rocks on one side of the fault. The rocks are thus caused to slide a little way and to release some of the pressure that is building up. A problem facing the scientists, however, is determining how much water is needed to cause a desirable, small rock slippage.

Perhaps the most interesting aspects of the science of earthquakes are those things that we do not yet understand. People who are caught in an earthquake often report sights and sounds that scientists cannot explain. For example, you have read about several reports of waves passing through the ground or through other solid objects as the earthquake shocks pass. These waves have been described as looking much like "swells in ocean water" and, when they are in the ground, seem to be coming from the direction of the source of the earthquake. Earthquakes do send out waves through the earth, of course, but these waves are traveling at thousands of miles-per-hour and it seems unlikely that they could be seen.

Similar waves have reportedly been seen traveling along pavement and up and down smoke stacks and chimneys made of brick. One scientist was in his California laboratory during an earthquake and watched what he described as waves six

A large sign in English and Arabic stands above the wreckage of the modern Saada Hotel which was destroyed by an earthquake in 1960.

inches high ripple through the concrete floor. After the quake, he examined the floor with a magnifying glass and found no new cracks at all! It has been suggested that the seeing of waves like these is an optical illusion caused by the violent movement of the fluid in the ears of the person caught in the earthquake.

Many of the sounds that people hear during an earthquake can be easily explained. Buildings that are being shaken creak and crack. Trees sway violently and their branches snap and groan. Water and air are pushed from loose soil by the shaking. But other sounds are more difficult to explain. Steady roaring sounds "coming from beneath the earth" are often described. And a few people have reported hearing the roaring of the earthquake *before* the earth beneath them begins to shake. Dogs, cats, and other animals sometimes seem to be able to sense the coming of an earthquake, sometimes several hours before the shaking is felt by human beings.

But the most difficult question about earthquakes that scientists must answer is, "What causes earthquakes?" We know, of course, that earthquakes are caused when rocks slip along faults. But why do the rocks slip? Where does the pressure that pushes them come from?

This mystery may be about to be solved. Geologists have recently developed a new understanding of the crust of the earth that leads them to believe that perhaps earthquakes, volcanoes, and mountains are all caused by the same forces within the earth. As you have seen as you read this book, most earthquakes occur in the same regions of the earth in which volcanoes are usually found. And these regions are located near mountains that have only recently in the history of the earth been pushed up from the sea.

Putting together a great deal of evidence from many sources, geologists have developed a new theory about how our earth got the face that it has. According to this theory, the earth's surface is divided into segments called *plates*.

No one can be certain at this time how many plates the earth's surface is divided into. Although some scientists think that there may be as many as 20 or more, most experts agree that there are at least six to eight major plates. One plate contains all of Europe and Asia. Another underlies almost all of the Pacific Ocean. A third plate contains Africa. A fourth is under the Indian Ocean and includes the land areas of Australia and India. A fifth major plate includes Antarctica and much of the nearby ocean. North America and the Arctic region are on the same plate, which extends eastward to the center of the Atlantic Ocean. Some geologists feel that the South American Continent is on the same plate, while others draw their maps in such a way as to show South America and the western part of the South Atlantic Ocean to be on a separate, seventh plate.

How many plates there actually are is not very important to us right now. The important thing is that at least some of them are actually moving.

Like huge rafts, thousands of miles across and between 20 and 100 miles deep, the plates seem to be floating on the almost-liquid rocks below. The movement is, as you might expect, very slow—perhaps only an inch or so a year at the most. But when we look at a map of the plates and a map of the major earthquake belts of the earth, there is a remarkable similarity. The earthquake belts of the earth occur at or close to the edges of the major plates—where they meet. In the North Atlantic, for example, most earthquakes occur along the Mid-Atlantic Ridge, the boundary of the North American Plate and the Eurasian Plate. Not only do earthquakes occur along the Mid-Atlantic Ridge, but volcanoes also are common on the Ridge. In fact most of the earth's volcanoes and major mountain ranges seem to occur along the edges of these plates. So, perhaps, even the very slow movement of some of the major plates of the earth's surface can help us to explain earthquakes, volcanoes, and even mountain building.

For example, let us consider the plate upon which North America rides. This huge piece of the earth's crust extends from the Mid-Atlantic Ridge to the western edge of the continent. On its western edge, along the west coast of the United States and Canada, this plate touches the huge plate upon which the Pacific Ocean rests. The North American Plate is being pushed steadily toward the west. The Pacific Plate, on the other hand, seems to be moving in a north-westerly

Reelfoot Lake, Tennessee, was formed by the New Madrid, Missouri, earthquake in 1811. The forest land sank so low that water filled in the hollow.

In Montana, the Hebgen Lake earthquake in 1959 split the earth leaving steps two feet high in this nearby highway.

direction. What must happen where these two plates meet?

Some geologists think that the North American Plate is overriding the edge of the Pacific Plate. As the two plates grind against each other, these scientists suggest, the edge of the Pacific Plate is forced deeper and deeper beneath North America. At the same time, the western edge of the North American Plate is pushed slightly upward. As this happens, the rocks of the upper plate fold and fault.

One result of this type of movement would be the formation of mountains. We might picture the mountains that line the western edge of the American continents as being wrinkles in the crust of the earth caused by the pressure of one plate's edge against that of its neighbor.

Another result of this kind of movement would certainly be earthquakes. The edge of the North American Plate does not follow the coastline exactly, but swings inland somewhere between Los Angeles and San Francisco. Apparently, then, Los Angeles rides on the edge of the Pacific Plate and is moving slowly toward the northwest. San Francisco, on the other hand, sits on the edge of the North American Plate and is being pushed almost due west. The edges of these two plates are marked by the mountains of the coast and by the hundreds of faults that crisscross the area. As the plates push against each other pressure builds higher and higher. Sooner or later this pressure becomes too great and the plates suddenly slip a little. The result is an earthquake.

If we accept the theory of plates we can answer the question of where the pressure comes from that causes earthquakes. But now we are faced with an even more difficult question. Where does the pressure come from that moves the *plates*? It would require a tremendous amount of energy to move even the smallest of the earth's plates even a fraction of an inch. What a gigantic force it must take to move an entire continent and half an ocean!

Geologists think they may have an answer to this question, too. It is a well-accepted idea that the interior of the earth is very, very hot. Actually, it seems likely that the temperatures of the rocks deep within the earth are higher than the melting point of the rocks. But the rocks are probably not liquid because of the tremendous pressure from the weight of the rocks above them. Therefore, scientists assume that these deep rocks do not flow like a liquid does. But they probably would change shape slowly if uneven pressure were put on them.

So we can picture the material upon which the plates rest as being made up of almost-liquid rock that is very hot. Now suppose that one section of this rock becomes heated more than the other sections around it. This overheated rock would expand and take up more space. Each cubic foot of the expanded rock would weigh less than it did before, since it now contains less material. The less dense rock would then slowly—very, very slowly—start to rise toward the surface.

As it neared the surface, the pressure on the rock would become less and less and it would become more liquid. If the liquid came in contact with a fault, a volcano would be produced and lava would be forced out onto the surface. This, scientists suggest, would be the edge of a plate. The liquid rock would then spread out along both sides of the fault, cooling and becoming more dense as it moved away from the source of heat. As time passed, this material would be carried away from the fault as the plate moved. Being heavier now, it would eventually sink back into the earth, probably in one of the many *trenches* that cut the ocean floors around the earth.

It is this movement of material from inside the earth that is thought to carry the continents along. For example, it is suggested that the Mid-Atlantic Ridge is being formed by lava rising to the surface along a huge series of faults, and that the North American Plate is being carried westward by the current in the rocks. The plates that contain Europe and Africa are being carried toward the east by the material flowing from the Ridge.

These ideas are *hypotheses*, educated guesses based on much accumulated data. And we can be certain that many more interesting ideas will be suggested before the geologists agree that they understand the causes of earthquakes. Meanwhile, more studies of earthquakes are being made. And as a result of these studies, perhaps a better understanding of the causes and effects of earthquakes will come about. Then, someday, man may perhaps be able to predict, live with, and even control this tremendous force of nature.

HURRICANES

THE EYE OF THE STORM

CHIEF WARRANT OFFICER Ray Boylan looked up at the dark Florida sky as he walked from his car to the Fleet Weather Facility. Most of his 18 years in the Navy had been spent observing and predicting weather conditions, so it was only natural for him to notice the before-dawn clouds. He felt absent-mindedly among the many pockets of his flight suit to see if he had his car keys and his pipe. His thoughts were on today's mission. As Flight Meteorologist, it would be his job to guide a 132,000-pound plane and its 24-man crew into the center of a hurricane.

As Boylan stepped into the building with its familiar weather charts and maps lining the walls, Tex Meyers, the Hurricane Duty Officer, waved to him. Tex was talking on the telephone as he walked from one end of the long drafting table to the other. The long telephone cord dragged along behind him. He handed Boylan the Tropical Cyclone P.O.D. (Plan-of-the-Day) without interrupting his conversation. When there was a hurricane brewing, Tex often had to do more than one thing at a time. He had to take calls from the National Hurricane Center in Miami—calls that gave him in-formation to add to what he already had. He had to handle calls from people along the Atlantic and Gulf Coasts—people who wanted to know if the storm was expected to come inland. They were anxious to know where and when it might strike. This time of year it was common to see Tex calmly performing the many tasks at hand while talking on the phone with the long, stretched-out cord following his steps.

Boylan read the instructions for the crew he was to fly with. Although he had been told his assignment earlier, the P.O.D. from the National Hurricane Center in Miami was official and gave him detailed instructions. He was to gather weather information around, and in-side a hurricane that was moving toward the Florida Keys. This flight would go into the center, or the eye, of the hurricane two times before the plane returned to Jacksonville. The P.O.D. also told him exactly where the storm had been at midnight. Another message told him the lowest pressure in the center, how strong the winds were in and around the storm, and described the clouds in the area. It was Boylan's job to meet with the flight crew before takeoff time. He would tell them where they were to fly, what information they were to get, and what the weather conditions were expected to be. He would work with the pilot, the radar man, and the navigator to decide the best plan for entering the eye of the hurricane. It would also be his job later in the day to talk to the pilot on the plane's intercom and guide him under the heavy bank of clouds that is known as the "eyewall." He and his assistants would see that the in-formation called for in the P.O.D. was collected and sent back to ground weather stations. This information would include the exact position of the storm at noon and again at six o'clock that evening. They would radio back descriptions of the clouds and winds in and around the storm. They would take readings of air pressure and the amount of moisture in the air.

GETTING THE PLANE READY

After the crew briefing, the plane was loaded and checked. There was food to be put on board. Weather instruments had to be loaded that would later be dropped from the plane during flight. The weather instruments and equipment that stayed on the plane had to be checked. In addition, flight instruments, fuel tanks, tires, landing gears—the whole plane—required last-minute inspection.

They were flying a Super Constellation C-121. It was an older plane that was once used for commercial flights. In fact, it was just such a plane in which Wilbur Wright, at the age of 72, had made his last flight. That had been in 1944. The crew sometimes flew in a newer plane, a WP 3A Orion. They looked forward to the time when all of their planes would be Orions because they could fly faster and get to the storm area in less time.

Now the plane was "geared up" for hurricane flying. The pilot, copilot, and flight engineer were in the very front of the plane. Behind them were bunks and seats for nonduty crew members, a very small kitchen (called a galley) and radio, radar, and other navigating equipment. The meteorological station was toward the rear of the plane.

This huge hulk of a plane has four engines that together deliver 13,000 horsepower—more than eight

The Hurricane Hunters like this aircraft, a WP 3A Orion, because it can get them to storms faster than the old Super Constellations.

locomotives. Enough electricity is generated to light a town of 3,000 people. The plane can carry 8,500 gallons of fuel, which is enough to last 22 hours of flight time. When it is fully loaded, the aircraft can weigh as much as 145,000 pounds.

As the crew prepared the plane for takeoff, the morning sun began to give a continuous change of color to the low-hanging clouds. The St. Johns River reflected this color as the fire-red changed to orange-pink and then to a pale seashell pink. Then it was daylight. The men had been on hand since 4 a.m. They had a long day ahead of them and a possibly dangerous mission to perform. But there was nothing about their behavior that would make you think this was expected to be anything more than an ordinary weather investigation flight. From their calmness they might have been civilians working on the 91st floor of an office building, not

The force of hurricane winds can be strong enough to cause a house to collapse.

Navy Hurricane Hunters about to fly at altitudes of only 500 to 1,500 feet above the sea. These men, dressed in special flight suits, were attentive to their instruments and equipment, and efficient in their motions.

While other crew members were busy, Commander Aschenbeck sat in the pilot's seat, his hands turning switches on and off, his eyes reading dials, his ears listening to the sounds of the engines and the voice of the copilot, Lt. J. H. Scattergood. Scattergood started to read off a list of things that had to be checked before takeoff. Once Commander Aschenbeck and his plane were off the ground and over water, there was not too much for the crew to do—not until they got closer to the storm, which was several hours away as yet.

Some of the off-duty or slow time is spent in training. This makes it possible for men who are new to this kind of flight to learn their duties from the more experienced crew members. For instance, Ray Boylan spent a whole year working with another flight meteorologist before taking over the position of "metro" on his own. Even though he had years of experience and training in meteorology before being assigned to the Hurricane Hunters, he still needed special instruction and experience for this particular kind of mission. And like other crew members, he got that training by working with an experienced crew, doing routine oceanographic studies as well as tracking hurricanes.

During times of the year when hurricanes are not likely to occur, the plane and crew fly into winter storms over the North Atlantic. Or sometimes they investigate the smooth waters between Cape Hatteras and the Bermudas. In any case, they always take readings from their weather instruments and radio the information back to a ground station. The meteorologists at the National Meteorological Center in Washington, D.C., use the information to help them make weather predictions.

There are several instruments that hang down from the underside of the back part of the plane. One of these uses infrared light rays to sense the temperature of the water below. This temperature is recorded inside the plane.

The temperature of the water below the surface can be measured by a BT, which stands for bathythermograph. The BT is dropped from the plane and floats on the water. A thin wire carries a temperature-sensing element down through the water at a rate of three hundred feet per minute. Inside the BT, the salt water from the sea starts a battery that supplies power for sending a radio signal back to the plane. This radio signal changes according to the temperature of the water below. Inside the plane, there is a special recorder for the radio signal. After the below-surface water temperatures are taken, a water-soluble seal on the BT dissolves and the instrument fills with water and sinks.

All of the information that can be gathered about the ocean and the air around the plane is fed into a machine that collects information located inside the plane. This machine can record and send by way of radio teletype 30 pieces of information. This tells the ground station when the readings were taken, the exact position of the plane, which direction it was headed and at what speed. It records, among other things, the wind speed and direction, the air pressure, the air temperature,

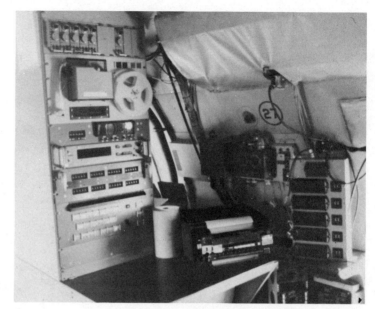

The Navy's meteorologist uses this equipment on the plane to gather information about a hurricane.

the temperature of the sea's surface, and a description of the clouds.

As the plane got closer to the storm, the meteorologist watched the surface of the sea from a bubble window next to his seat. He could see the changes in the waves of the water beneath them as the wind increased. When they left Jacksonville, the water had only occasional ripples and no whitecaps. This was because there was very little surface wind. As the wind increased, there were a few whitecaps. Now and then, as the whitecaps increased in size and frequency, one would become wider and be carried downwind. Boylan knew the wind speed was about 10 to 12 knots per hour (about 13 miles per hour) from looking at the behavior of the water. As the wind increased to 18 knots (21 miles per hour), there were slight streaks on the water, parallel to the wind direction. Whitecaps and patches of foam covered the entire sea.

The flight meteorologist, or metro, as his teammates call him, keeps the pilot and crew informed as to the changing weather conditions. He and his assistants make reports to be radioed back to the ground weather stations. The ground station in Jacksonville needs the weather data being sent back, but they have another reason for keeping radio communication with the plane. They want to be sure the crew is safe. If they don't receive a report from the plane every half hour, they send a message to the plane. If they get no answer on their assigned radio frequency, they try other frequencies. If an hour and a half should go by without hearing from the plane, a search and rescue mission is planned. Such a mission is not actually carried out until the plane has had time to use all its fuel, or until the ground station receives more information.

Boylan remembers one time when the radio on his plane wasn't working right. It could receive messages, but it couldn't send them. The crew could hear the calls from Jacksonville, but couldn't let the ground station know they were all right. They heard the first routine calls, and then they could hear the concern in the voice of the radioman in Jacksonville as he tried to get through to the plane and failed to get an answer.

Of course, they weren't lost or in trouble. But they were glad to know that someone was keeping an eye on them—just in case they should need help someday.

ENTERING THE STORM'S EYE

When they were close enough to the storm, the plane's radar equipment gave them a good view of the cloud pattern around the eye of the hurricane. The pilot, metro, navigator, and radar officer studied this pattern and decided which would be the best way to enter the eye. The reflection of the clouds on the radar screen showed the almost-clear eye surrounded by a circle of clouds. Leading into this circle from the surrounding area were finger-like clouds, called feeder bands. These clouds curved around the storm, making the picture on the radar screen look like a giant pinwheel.

Hurricanes have two kinds of motion. In the northern hemisphere, winds within a hurricane always blow around an area of low pressure in a counter clockwise direction. This gives the storm a circular pattern. In addition, the storm as a whole moves across the water. The direction of this motion is not always the same. In order to predict the path the storm will take, Navy or Air Force planes fly into the eye of the storm every six hours and locate its point of lowest air pressure. By marking this spot on a map they are able to follow the direction the storm is moving and to know when it makes a change in direction. Using this information, meteorologists can make a good guess as to where the storm will go next. They can warn ships at sea to stay clear of that area. They can prepare people on land to be ready for the possibility of winds and rain that can destroy property and take lives.

Commander Aschenbeck looked at the radar screen as he talked to the radar officer, the navigator, and the metro. It was at this point that he had to decide whether or not to enter the eye of the storm. Navy regulations forbid entering a storm center at a low level where the eye is less than 15 miles in diameter. Another condition for the low-level entrance is that the winds within the storm must not be reported or be predicted to be greater than 120 knots (138 miles per hour). In addition, both of the plane's radar systems have to be working properly. The safety of the crew is the most important consideration in the decision of whether or not to enter the storm.

The four men studied the cloud pattern. The calm eye appeared to be about 25 miles across, and the wind speeds were last reported to be about 90 knots. In addition, there was a thin spot in the clouds surrounding the eye—it looked like a good place to make the entrance.

They decided the best path on which to fly into the storm would be between the trailing cloud bands. The clear space between the bands would not be so rough to fly in, and they could stay at a higher altitude and still see the water. After they flew closer to the eye, they would run out of clear space between the clouds and have to drop down under the clouds. Once the pilot made the decision to go ahead and enter the storm center, it was the metro's job to guide the plane safely in.

As they moved in toward the eye of the storm, the pressure altimeter could no longer be used to tell them how high above the water the plane was flying. This instrument makes its altitude readings from the air pressure. Under ordinary flying conditions this is a good instrument to use. But the expected drop in air pressure in the center of a hurricane would cause the pressure

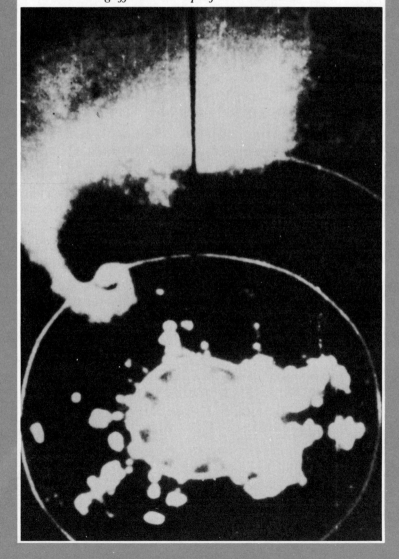

Radar screen showing the reflection of the "hooked finger" of a tornado. The lower part of the picture shows reflection of the radar waves bouncing off the raindrops of a thunderstorm.

altimeter to give a false reading. There are two other kinds of altitude-measuring instruments on the plane—a radar altimeter and a radio altimeter. These instruments direct radar pulses or radio waves to the surface below. They automatically calculate the distance above the surface by how long it takes for the signals to hit the ground or water below and bounce back to the plane.

The radio altimeter can be read on a screen by one of the metro's assistants. This screen is black, and the altitude reading is seen on it as a green line that wiggles as the plane bounces or changes altitude. You can understand why this altimeter is called the Green Worm.

When the plane got close to the storm, the pilot ordered everyone to fasten his seat belt. All crewmen were to put on their life vests. It was necessary for one of the metro's assistants to be able to move about in the plane to take readings from weather instruments. Everyone else and everything on the plane was tied down so the men would not be injured by objects flying about inside the plane as the flight got rougher. As the turbulence increased, the men in the pilot's area had to work harder to keep the plane steady and on its course. They needed information from the radar officer and the navigator to tell them if they were on the proper course.

Eventually, the space between the cloud bands disappeared, and it was necessary to drop down under the clouds to keep the water below in sight. Boylan's view from his bubble window was the only one of any use. Up front, the pilot and copilot could see only the heavy sheet of rain surging down over the windows. They guided the plane partially by reading the dials on their instruments, but mostly they were kept on the right track by voice communication with the radar officer and the metro.

Every 30 seconds the pilot could hear the metro's assistant give a "green worm" altitude reading.

Green worm, seven fifty.

Then the radar man followed with,

Your heading is good; eyewall bearing zero three zero degrees, thirty miles ahead.

The metro would then give the pilot readings from his instruments. As he looked out his bubble window at the wave motion below, he would report the surface wind speed and wind direction. This was followed by—

Green worm, six hundred.

And then the pilot let him know he had heard and understood:

Roger.

Then from the navigator:

Drift two two degrees right.

At this point the rain that surrounded them became so heavy that the radar officer told the pilot,

I've lost the picture. I no longer have the eyewall. Recommend Metro take the conn. ("Take the conn" means to take over telling the pilot which direction to turn.)

The metro's voice came through:

Roger, I have the conn.

and the pilot said,

Roger, Metro has the conn.

This was punctuated by:

Green worm, five fifty.

By now the pilot had turned the switch that allowed everyone on the plane to hear what was being said by those controlling and guiding the plane. Those men who had no duties to perform during this tense period when they were entering the eye felt more comfortable knowing what was going on.

Boylan kept a constant watch on the sea surface. His voice and the green worm reading formed a continuous patter of information interspersed by the pilot's "Roger" and the navigator's voice giving them their headings and the route they could take in case they suddenly needed to turn back.

Green worm, five hundred.

Roger.

Flight metro recommends come port two zero degrees. Surface winds two two zero degrees ninety-five knots.

Green worm, four fifty.

Your escape heading is one zero zero degrees. (This came from the navigator.)

Roger, one zero zero degrees.

The metro helped the pilot keep the plane headed directly into the center of the storm by seeing that the wind was always blowing straight in toward the plane on its left side. This is because the winds inside the storm blow in a counter clockwise direction. If you could stand outside the eye, facing the center of the storm, the wind would always be blowing against your left side. Using this information, the metro could tell the pilot when they were drifting off course by watching the wind action on the water below.

Metro has lost sight of the water. Drop down.

Green worm, four hundred.

I have surface contact now.

Green worm, steady at four hundred.

Roger.

Up front, the sounds of the engines were drowned out by the thunderous noise of the unbelieveably heavy rainfall. The plane was tossed about as they flew just over the water. Since the pilot's chair is adjustable, it is not very steady, and it jiggled as the plane vibrated. So it was very difficult for the pilot to read the dials on the instrument panels.

At one time or another the motion caused some of

Waves, pushed ahead of the hurricane, often do more damage than the winds that follow.

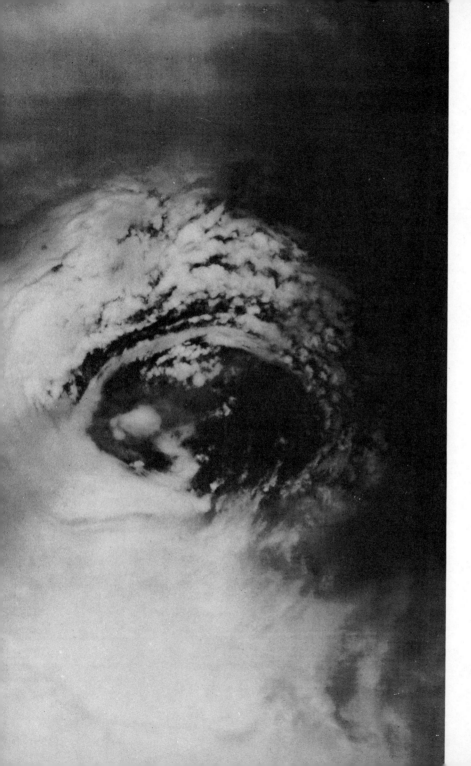

the crew members to become airsick. Each of them had a plastic-lined paper bag close at hand. If a man got sick, he used the bag and then resumed his work. The voices continued over the intercom.

Green worm, four hundred.
Steady on flight. Surface winds two eight zero degrees at one hundred ten knots.
Green worm, three seventy-five.
Roger, green worm.

INSIDE THE EYE

Suddenly the turbulence ceased. The plane had broken through the eyewall. Up front, Aschenbeck could hear the plane's engines again and see out the window. The instrument panel was clearly readable. The plane was out of the rain. They were no longer in the storm, but they were surrounded by it. They were in the eye of the hurricane. The men were aware of the rivulets of perspiration that covered them. Their flight suits were made of a special flame-resistant material, for safety's sake, and were normally very warm to wear. But today they seemed to be warmer than usual—perhaps because of the tenseness they felt while coming under the eyewall of the storm.

The metro's job now changed. He no longer was needed for guiding the pilot under the clouds.

Now he had to see that the weather information was collected accurately and sent back to the ground station. Boylan requested the navigator to take a reading of their position. This was radioed back to the ground station. Next the plane flew back and forth across the center of the storm to find the spot of lowest air pressure—this was also marked on their map and radioed back with other readings from the meteorological instruments.

Inside the eye, Aschenbeck adjusted his colored glasses against the glare and looked out the window on his left. He remembered his first flight into a storm center and how surprised he had been that the eye was not clear. There were lots of white fluffy clouds, making it difficult to see very far. They circled close to the eyewall, the bank of clouds that had presented such a challenge coming in. It was a boundary line between them and the wild winds of the hurricane. Looking below, the pilot could see under the bank of clouds, back into the turbulent area they had just come through. The surface of the water was frothy there, like whipped egg whites. Inside the eye, the water surface danced in small peaks.

There were almost always birds inside the eye of a storm. Perhaps they had been caught there and swept along with the storm. Or maybe they were blown in before the storm became so severe. At any rate they were not strong enough to escape. If they could have crossed the eyewall, the winds and hard rains on the other side would have destroyed them. So they flew around inside the eye. Sometimes they collided with airplanes there. It was impossible for the pilot to maneuver the plane so as to miss them. He could only hope one wouldn't crash through the front window, or damage an engine or the tail section.

You might expect the crew to feel a lift in spirits, relieved at having the most dangerous part of the mission over. And they did feel the tension go as they performed routine tasks inside the eye. But they knew their orders called for leaving the eye and then entering it a second time that day. That entrance would come in exactly six hours.

STILL WORK TO BE DONE

After they had radioed information regarding their position and weather instrument readings, they flew back out of the eye the same way they had come in. Only this time the feelings of tension were not so great as entering the eye. The turbulence become less intense instead of greater as they flew away from the eye. On the way out they took more readings of temperature, air pressure, wind force and direction, dew point, and water temperature.

For several hours after the plane left the hurricane, it flew around the storm, gathering routine information about the ocean and the air. The plane made its second entrance into the center of the storm so that it would fall six hours after they had entered it the first time. They recorded and radioed back the information that was needed and headed out of the eye again—this time they were going home.

On the flight back to the base, some of the men who did not have duties to perform played cards or talked. Some read. But most of them slept. The bunks were a welcome sight to men who had been under the strain of getting the most information out of the trip and at the same time keeping themselves and their crewmates alive in a dangerous situation.

Because of the courage and dedication of these men, weather forecasters back on land would be able to give information to the public that could save many lives.

THE LONG ISLAND EXPRESS SEPTEMBER, 1938

THE HURRICANE SEASON of 1938 had not been a particularly bad one for the United States. In New England the late summer months had been a little too warm to be really comfortable. In mid-September the air had become damp and sticky. Three hurricanes had smashed their way into the Gulf of Mexico. The first had died quietly in the Florida Straits on August 10. A second had crossed the coastline and caused $250,000 damage to property in Louisiana. The third was stronger, but died quickly over the dry deserts of central Mexico, after causing only a little damage along the coast of Yucatan. These storms were too far away to be of much interest to the people living in the states north of New York City.

The fourth hurricane of the season caught the Brazilian ship the *SS Alegrete* on September 16. At the time, the *Alegrete* was about halfway between the coast of Africa and the West Indies—that string of islands that separates the Atlantic Ocean from the Caribbean Sea. While being tossed by tremendous waves, the little ship managed to send out a warning.

"Winds of hurricane strength," it reported. "Barometer reading of 28.31 inches."

No one knows exactly how a hurricane begins, or where this particular one started. One guess is that the low pressure area was first created over a super-heated part of the Sahara Desert some 10 or 12 days before it smashed into the *Alegrete* in the mid-Atlantic. Above the hot sand, the air would have become more and more heated. As it did so it would have expanded and risen upward rapidly. Cooler air, rushing into the low pressure area left by the rising air, would have been thrown into a whirling motion by the spinning of the earth.

On each side of the equator is a band of steadily flowing air called the Trade Winds. Blowing roughly from the northeast toward the southwest, these winds blew the little whirlwind over the desert, across the western coast of Africa, and out to sea. Fed by warm, moist air over the water, the storm grew in strength, and by the time it reached the Cape Verde Islands, some 400 miles west of the African coast, it had become strong enough to be called a gale (winds of more than 40 miles per hour). We can assume that it reached hurricane strength—winds of 75 miles per hour or more—somewhere just west of the Cape Verde Islands.

For several days the hurricane acted as expected. It continued to move toward the west at about 20 miles per hour. It gathered up tons of warm water vapor from the Atlantic below it. This water vapor was carried upward by the rising air currents around the center of the storm. As the air spiraled upward it became cooler and the water vapor condensed back into liquid water and then froze into ice crystals. These changes in the state of the water—from a vapor to a liquid and then to a solid—released tremendous amounts of heat energy that drove the winds faster.

On September 19, the hurricane seemed to threaten the east coast of Florida as it began to curve slightly toward the northwest. All along that coast, hurricane-wise people made preparations for the storm. Small boats were taken from the water and larger ones were anchored more firmly. Boards were nailed over glass windows. On the off-shore islands and in the lower areas of the mainland, people packed their most valuable possessions and began to stream toward higher ground.

But this was one storm that was not going to bother the citizens of Florida. Directly ahead of the storm's center and to the north of it were two areas of very high pressure that were to change it from a normal Caribbean hurricane into the most damaging storm ever to hit the New England states.

Severe hurricanes rarely strike the Atlantic coast north of New York City. Tropical storms usually either move inland long before they reach New England and lose their strength, or they swing back out into the North Atlantic and die over its cold water.

But the weather maps for mid-September showed two masses of cool, heavy air. One of these high pressure areas was shaped like an egg and covered all of central North America from Dallas, Texas, to Hudson Bay, north of Canada. The second high pressure area was the stronger of the two—that is, the pressure of its air was greater. It lay near Newfoundland's Great Banks, nearly 1,000 miles east of the New England coast.

Between these two highs was a long, narrow corridor

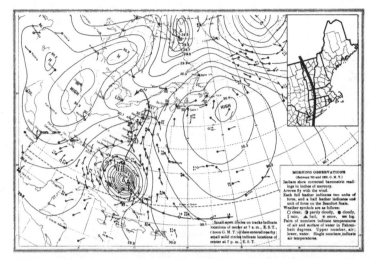

This weather map shows two high-pressure areas forming the low-pressure trough that led The Long Island Express directly towards New England.

of lower pressure that the meteorologists call a trough. This particular trough lay almost directly over the east coast of the United States, from just east of Florida to northern New England. As the storm reached the entrance to the trough it paused briefly. Then the hurricane turned into the low pressure trough and headed north. At this time the storm's center was just north of Haiti and the Dominican Republic, moving forward at only 15 miles per hour. The date was September 19.

The hurricane followed the trough northward. At 7 a.m. on the twentieth, the Washington Weather Bureau announced that the storm's center was 300 miles east-northeast of Miami and that its speed was increasing. Storm warnings were issued for the entire Atlantic coast.

150

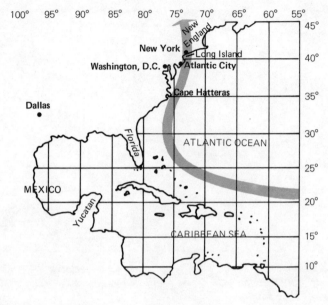

The path of The Long Island Express, 1938.

Warning flags were hoisted in Eastport, Maine, that showed that a strong wind was expected from the *northeast*. Apparently, the Weather Bureau scientists had guessed that the storm would curve back toward the east and miss the coast line entirely.

The next morning, the report from the weather station at Cape Hatteras, North Carolina, noted winds of 50 miles per hour were coming from the northwest. This showed that the center of the storm lay to the northeast of Hatteras. At that time, the barometer at Hatteras gave a nearly normal reading of 29.30 inches. At the very center of the storm the pressure was nearly 1.25 inches lower than the Hatteras reading, so we can assume that the storm stood many miles out to sea from the weather station.

The people who lived along the coast south of New York City were warned to expect gale-force winds. Small boats were taken in, fishing trips cancelled, and larger boats moved to safer harbors. In New England, the flags still warned only of a coming storm with winds of less than 40 miles per hour.

That was at 7 a.m. on September 21. At 1 p.m. the Atlantic City, New Jersey, weather station reported winds of over 60 miles per hour coming from the west and a barometric pressure of less than 29 inches. In those six hours, between 7 a.m. and 1 p.m., the storm had moved nearly 300 miles. Moving like an express train, the hurricane rushed toward the unsuspecting people of the New England states.

In the 300 years since the pilgrims landed at Plymouth Rock, only eight damaging hurricanes had reached these states before 1938. Nearly 70 years had passed since the New England coast has suffered a major tropical storm, and many of the citizens of the region felt that they were safe from what they called "Florida hurricanes." Newspapers printed in Worcester, Massachusetts, for distribution on the morning of September 21, carried the prediction that the winds would be strong but gave no warning that a hurricane was coming.

Shortly after noon on September 21, the hurricane claimed its first human lives. As the storm swept northward at 50 miles an hour, it pushed a large storm wave nearly 100 miles ahead of it. In front of the storm, on the beaches of Long Island, the sun shone dimly through thin clouds that raced toward the northwest. But there was no rain. Brave swimmers fought with the stronger-than-normal surf while others watched from the beach. Then, as the waves passed the usual high tide mark, the swimmers left the water and the lower beach for the safety of 12-foot-high dunes behind the beach. Suddenly, without any real warning, an 18-foot storm wave smashed Long Island like a battering ram and swept its beaches clear. The swimmers who thought they stood safely on the high sand dunes were washed out to sea as the wave retreated.

Everyone had been caught by surprise. The storm, if it had followed the pattern of the normal hurricane, should have been nearly 200 miles to the south, moving sluggishly along at about 20 miles per hour. Instead, it now swept the beaches of Long Island and roared inland at a speed that at one time reached over 60 miles per hour. Because it moved as fast as a train, the hurricane was later nicknamed "The Long Island Express."

Warnings were too late to be of help to the people of Long Island, and for some reason the people living to the north of New York City were not told of the dangerous nature of the storm. By two o'clock the winds over the eastern section of Long Island reached more than 70 miles per hour. Telephone poles and lines were down everywhere. At Quogue Village, only 12 out of 180 houses stood after the storm had passed. At Sag Harbor, the steeple of the Presbyterian Church swayed, snapped, and fell. Montauk was completely cut off from the rest of the island.

Suddenly, at the very height of the storm, it became calm. To the stunned survivors the wind seemed to disappear, although it actually continued to blow at about 20 miles per hour. The eye of the storm was 40 miles in diameter and took more than half an hour to cross Long Island. And then the winds returned, now blowing from the opposite direction. Again the wind, rain, and tides smashed the already ruined Long Island, as if they could do more damage than had already been done.

The western half of the Connecticut shoreline was protected from the storm wave by Long Island. But to the east of the city of New London, the beaches of Connecticut and Rhode Island were swept by the same huge waves that had racked Long Island. These long, heavy waves smashed against the New England shore with such gigantic force that they caused the entire North American continent to shudder. On the Pacific Coast, 3,000 miles away, earthquake-recording machines called seismographs clearly showed the shock of each wave. Ships and boats were torn from their moorings and hurled ashore. Entire fleets of fishing boats were lost. Elsewhere along the coast, railroad tracks and trains were tossed around like driftwood, and dozens of small towns were destroyed. After crushing the houses, boats, and trains into a single tangled mass, the water rushed back into the Sound. The undertow that it created completed the devastation that the waves had begun, washing much of the debris and many bodies out to sea.

Even though protected somewhat from the high water, the western part of the Connecticut shore did not escape entirely. The center of the storm struck directly at New Haven, following winds of more than 120 miles per hour. The eye of the storm passed over the city at a few minutes before 4 p.m., and the barometers there recorded a low pressure of 28.11 inches.

The center of the storm charged straight north across the states of Connecticut, Massachusetts, and Vermont. Then it disappeared into Quebec, Canada. The most highly damaged area, however, was to the east of the storm's center. Here the winds blew strongly from the south toward the north as they circled in a counterclockwise direction around the eye. Added to the normal speed of the wind caused by the very low pressure of the hurricane's center was the forward motion of the storm, which was still more than 50 miles per hour. Many stations to the east of the path of the hurricane recorded winds of around 100 miles per hour over five minute periods. Blue Hill Weather Observatory, near Boston, recorded an average wind speed of 121 miles per hour over five minutes. Gusts of 150 to 185 miles per hour must have been common, however. Judging from the damage, some engineers believe that wind speeds of 250 miles per hour must have been reached in some places.

At 150 miles per hour the wind pushes with a force of 58 pounds per square foot. At 200 miles per hour the wind's pressure is more than 100 pounds per square foot. Throughout New England, trees, telephone poles, and transmission towers were sheared off by the wind. Houses lost their roofs and then collapsed. People were killed by pieces of glass, bricks, and lumber that flew through the air with the speed of bullets. After the wind passed, fires often broke out within the destroyed towns, completing the destruction.

The worst effect of almost every hurricane is flooding.

This is often true even far inland. It had rained heavily throughout New England during the four days before the storm, and the streams were full. No one was able to measure accurately the fall of rain during the hurricane, since winds of 50 miles per hour or more blow the falling rain almost horizontally, parallel with the ground. But tons of water must have fallen on New England during the afternoon. The Connecticut River rose rapidly out of its banks at Hartford, Connecticut. There the people tried to make sandbag levees but finally had to desert their town to the rushing water. Twelve feet of water filled Franklin Square in Norwich, Connecticut. In Springfield, Massachusetts, the wind whipped up eight-foot-high waves in the Connecticut River that washed through the city's streets.

Providence, Rhode Island, to the east of the storm's center, was hit by a different type of flood wave. Providence sits at the top of a long, narrow bay. The 100-mile-an-hour wind blowing directly up Narragansett Bay held the high tide there until the next tide moved in. Tide piled upon tide, and the overloaded streams added water to the bay until, in places, the water washed ashore 25 feet above the highest point water had ever reached before. This tidal wave flooded the streets of the city at almost exactly 5 p.m., when the unsuspecting citizens of Providence were on their way home after work. Many people were crushed as buildings collapsed. Others were killed by flying debris. Still others drowned in the city's streets.

As hurricanes move inland, they begin to lose strength quickly. The friction between the land and the air slows the speed of the wind. In addition, the storm is deprived of the supply of new energy it gets when it is over warm water. Without energy being added to it, the hurricane becomes steadily weaker.

The damage the storm did was very great. Nearly 700 people died as a direct result of the wind and water. One hundred of these had lived on Long Island, and another 100 in Massachusetts. Connecticut lost almost 100 people also. Rhode Island was the hardest hit, with close to 400 people dying within a few hours. In addition, over 1,500 people were injured during the storm.

The value of the property damaged by the Long Island Express was tremendous. More than 100,000 people lost some or all of their property, including 26,000 automobiles. An estimated 18,000 miles of electric lines were destroyed and had to be replaced. There were 600,000 telephones out of service, and travel by road was impossible in large parts of six states. And 300 million trees were destroyed or damaged. Since lumbering and fruit production are so important to this part of the United States, the value of so many trees is impossible to estimate.

New Englanders had assumed until then that a hurricane was no threat to them. But when they looked around at the damage done, they realized that more was needed than just cleaning up the mess. They passed laws requiring sturdier buildings, especially near the sea. They built sea walls and dikes. The flood walls built along the Connecticut River around Hartford have protected the area from flooding ever since 1938.

They also demanded hurricane observing stations for the North Atlantic states. However, no one followed through on these demands. Soon World War II began and there was silence on the radios of the ships in the Atlantic. Hurricane warnings were neglected for more urgent business.

Height of the storm.

THE TRI-STATE TORNADO MARCH 18, 1925

TORNADOES, LIKE HURRICANES, are very unpredictable. It is not possible to say exactly what they will do. A study made several years ago by J. R. Martin shows how difficult it is to describe a typical tornado. Mr. Martin studied the records of 1,000 tornadoes and he found that their average forward speed is 45 miles per hour. But he also found that some storm funnels remained stationary for some time before they began to move. And he found a few storms that traveled at more than a mile per minute. As a general rule, also, tornadoes move from southwest to northeast, but storms moving in almost any direction can be found in the records. One Oklahoma tornado actually made a complete circle before it rushed off across the prairie toward the east. And, tornadoes making sudden U-turns are not unheard of.

The average length of the path of destruction of a tornado is a little over 13 miles, and the average width of this path is less than one-fourth of a mile. But many tornadoes are larger or smaller than this. The tornado that occurred on March 18, 1925, is an example of a tornado that is not "average."

The conditions of the atmosphere that triggered the Tri-State Tornado of 1925 began to form sometime in early March somewhere above the Arctic circle in Alaska. A large mass of cold, dry Arctic air gathered into a huge low pressure area and slowly began to move south-southwestward. It appeared on the weather maps for the first time on March 16, over Calgary, Alberta, Canada. During the next 36 hours it moved rapidly southward, reaching the Oklahoma-Texas border near Wichita Falls, Texas, by nightfall of March 17.

At about this time, the low pressure area ran head-on into a mass of warm, wet air that had drifted northward from the Gulf of Mexico. As a result, the low turned sharply and began moving toward the northeast. During the night it drifted across southern Oklahoma and the morning of March 18 found it located on the weather maps just a little north of Ft. Smith, Arkansas. A long trough of low pressure had formed, running from Lake Erie to southwestern Texas. Into this trough moved two flows of air—the one from the north was cold and dry; the other from the Gulf was hot and wet. These air masses spiraled into the low pressure trough, mingled together, and began to whirl around. During the next 12 hours, at least eight tornadoes were to form as a result. One of these started the notorious Tri-State Tornado on its way. This was perhaps the worst tornado that has ever occurred anywhere in the world.

The tornado struck the ground for the first time at about 1 p.m. in Reynolds County, Missouri, and began carving out a three-fourths-mile-wide path of total destruction as it moved toward the northeast. Houses and larger buildings collapsed, trees were torn up by the roots, and at least 11 people died as the storm smashed its way across Missouri toward the Mississippi

River. The Weather Bureau recorded a speed of nearly 60 miles per hour.

Across the river in Illinois, the tornado crushed the town of Gorham, killing 90 and injuring 200 people. It left the little community almost completely destroyed. The distance to Murphysboro was covered in minutes and the larger town had no warning of the disaster that rushed down on it at nearly a mile per minute. Only seconds after being struck, the city lay in ruins. Murphysboro had been a cluster of about 200 blocks of homes and buildings. Suddenly, more than 150 of these city blocks lay in ruins. In the wreckage were the bodies of 234 people, and another 800 required medical help. Eleven huge steam engines lay on their sides in the railroad yard. Fires broke out throughout the rubble and the volunteer fire department discovered that the town's water supply had also been destroyed. Before the day was over, 8,000 people found themselves homeless.

A few people near DeSoto, Illinois, saw the storm coming. A brakeman on an Illinois Central train said that he saw a dark cloud hanging over the little town. "There were two blinding flashes of lightning and a crash of thunder," he said later. "After that, there was nothing left."

F. M. Hewitt was in the town itself, and he described the sky as a "seething, boiling mass of clouds whose color constantly changed. From the upper portion came a roaring noise as of many trains. Below this cloud was a tapering dark cloud mass reaching earthward." This was apparently the nearest to a funnel that this storm ever produced.

Hewitt was out of doors when the storm hit. He

A tornado over the Dallas, Texas, skyline shows the funnel dipping down out of the parent cloud.

Sometimes tornado clouds drop two or more funnels at one time. "Tornado Alley" is an area of frequent tornado activity running from Texas through Oklahoma, Kansas and Iowa.

reported later that the sky became so dark that he could see for only a few feet in front of him. During the flash of a lightning bolt, he saw a small frame house some distance away. As he watched, the house seemed to disappear, "just as if it had been dynamited," he said. Hewitt survived the storm, even though he tried to find shelter in a wooden house that lay directly in the path of the storm. The house collapsed and Mr. Hewitt was lifted by the wind and dumped into the street. Here he waited out the storm by hanging onto a post. He survived unhurt.

Nearby, a mother lay in her bed with her two-week-old baby. She heard the roar of the storm and felt the house shake and lift, as if it were going to fly. Above her, the timbers of the roof creaked and cracked. Finally they gave way and crashed down around the helpless pair. Later, rescue teams found both unhurt, protected from the debris by the roof timbers that luckily fell across the bed in such a way as to leave a small space for the mother and baby.

But most of the people who lived in DeSoto were not as lucky as this. Nearly 100 bodies were found after the storm passed. Many of these had been torn apart and identification was made by jewelry worn by arms that were not attached to bodies. Other bodies were pierced by splinters of wood that had been driven into them by the wind with the force of rifle bullets.

The tornado had by this time traveled more than 100 miles on the ground and had killed over 200 people. But instead of growing weaker, its force seemed to become stronger. Near Zeigler, the Illinois Central Railroad bridge was lifted from its concrete pillars and dumped six feet away. A wooden church was twisted so that its back end moved 15 feet and nearby a frame house was turned halfway around from its original position.

West Frankfort, Illinois, was the largest town in the path of the storm. Its 20,000 residents had no warning of the death and destruction that had taken place just a few miles to the southwest of them. They were completely unprepared for the tremendous force of the winds that swept through the northwestern part of their city. Here 64 houses were destroyed in less than two minutes. One hundred twenty-seven people died. Small sticks and splinters of wood were later found driven through the wooden walls of houses. In the railroad yard, a 2×4 board was driven through the side of a metal railroad car. In the town, a 2×8 pine plank smashed into the wall of a house and was blown through the siding and through a 2×4 oak stud. Nearby, a large plank was blown into a tree so hard that it was driven into the trunk. Later, it was found that the plank was so firmly wedged into the tree that a man could stand on the end of the plank without pulling it free.

On and on across Illinois the tornado rushed. At one spot it picked up a huge grain binder and carried it a quarter of a mile. Later it gathered up a large touring car and blew it 225 feet through the air before smashing it to the ground. The storm smashed through a school, destroyed the building, picked up all 16 pupils and deposited them unhurt 150 yards away from the rubble of their school. After the storm had passed, a barber chair was found in a field miles away from the nearest barber shop. And a pair of trousers containing $95 was found 39 miles away from their unhurt owner.

Near Crossville, on the Illinois-Indiana border, straws were picked up from the fields and blown with such force that they were driven into tree trunks as if they had been nails.

Leaving 606 people dead in Illinois, and 11 dead in southeastern Missouri, the tornado moved into its third state, Indiana. Griffin, Indiana, was completely destroyed. Every house left was so badly damaged that the town offered no shelter to any of its inhabitants. Thirty-four people were killed.

No one in Indiana saw a funnel either. The cloud was evidently too close to the ground. The storm was described by survivors as "a fog rolling toward me," or "a black turbulent mass." At Princeton, Indiana, where 200 homes were destroyed and 200 people died, the storm was described as "a blackness moving across the southern part of the city."

In Princeton, T. H. Phillips sat in his office in the coal shop of the Southern Railroad with one of his fellow workers. Unaware of the storm's coming until the sky began to darken, the two men were completely unprepared. Suddenly, Phillips felt himself being lifted upward along with his chair and desk. A few moments later he found himself lying face downward in the mud of the railroad yard. Later, the second workman was found under a huge pile of coal, like Phillips, completely unhurt.

Across town, four miners were returning home from their jobs when their car suddenly began to bounce along the road. The doors popped open and all four men were pulled from the automobile as if by a huge, unseen hand. The wind carefully dropped them, un-hurt, alongside the road, but tore the car into little pieces and scattered it along several miles of roadway.

One man reported that he was sitting in a resturant, eating an early dinner, when the storm struck. "The roof went first, and then all four walls exploded outward," he recalled. "Suddenly, there I was, sitting on the floor, with nothing at all around me. That's when I left!"

Finally, after spending more than three hours on the ground, the tornado passed Princeton, Indiana. Behind it was a path of total destruction that averaged three-fourths of a mile wide and was 219 miles long. In this swath of rubble lay the bodies of 689 citizens of three states. Nearly 2,000 people had been injured by the storm and perhaps as many as 15,000 were left homeless. Four small towns were completely wiped off the map by the fury of the wind.

Fortunately, storms such as the Tri-State Tornado are very unusual. But the fact that a single tornado once stayed on the ground for such a long time and smashed across 100 square miles of land shows that it could happen again. However, with modern methods of warning, it is very unlikely that the death toll would be as high. The Tri-State Tornado killed its first victim at one o'clock in the afternoon and smashed into Princeton, Indiana, at 4:18 p.m. With the tornado warning system that is now used by the Weather Service along with the widespread use of television and radios, the people in the path of such a storm would today have enough notice to be able to move to safer ground. A tragedy such as the Tri-State Tornado is not likely to happen again.

WINDS
OF
DESTRUCTION

THE WEATHER—WHAT A tremendous influence it has on all of us! We wake up wondering what kind of day it will be. When people meet they almost always talk about the weather.

"Is it going to rain today?"

"Do I need to wear a warm coat?"

"We can't have a picnic today. The weather man is predicting heavy rains."

"I have never seen such a dry spell! I wish it would rain soon."

"We have to get this crop in before the rains start."

Living at the bottom of a deep ocean of air, we are all constantly affected in some way by the weather around us. Some groups of people are more concerned with the weather than others are. Farmers, whose crops depend upon the rainfall and temperature, watch the weather more closely than the office worker does. The construction worker may be more aware of changes in the weather that prevent him from working than the student in school is. And the people who live along the coast and on islands keep a close eye on any changes in the clouds above them during the hurricane season. The inhabitants of Tornado Alley also watch the sky as they go about their daily business during the months when tornadoes are likely to come rushing down upon them. Often these people look at the sky without consciously thinking about storms.

Man has always felt he was at the mercy of the weather. Ancient people everywhere assumed that, since they could not control the weather, rains and drought were controlled by the gods. They made elaborate ceremonies to please their gods. They thought that when men and property were destroyed by storms it was because the gods had become angry with them.

We have not known that the weather "moved" for very long. A windstorm was either assumed to happen everywhere at once, or it was thought to occur in only a single place and then to disappear. Benjamin Franklin once wanted to travel to Boston from Philadelphia to watch an eclipse of the moon. He was unable to travel because of a very bad storm. Later he was surprised to learn that Boston had been very clear and the eclipse had been easily seen. He was even more surprised to learn that Boston had suffered a severe storm the day after the eclipse. Franklin suggested that perhaps it was the same storm, moving slowly across the country from Philadelphia to Boston. Franklin's friend, Thomas Jefferson, kept a careful diary of weather conditions for many years. These observers helped later scientists to learn a great deal about the weather and its causes.

We now know that the atmosphere nearest Earth's surface is in constant motion and that it moves in large patterns. The air near the equator receives more heat from the sun than does the air in cooler climates. This warming by the sun causes the air to expand. As it expands, it becomes lighter and floats upward and then moves either north or south. At the poles, the air is cool-

This fishing trawler was hurled by hurricane winds into someone's front yard in Biloxi, Mississippi (above). Tornado winds were so strong they imbedded a piece of wood into a piece of steel.

er. Therefore it is heavier and settles down to the level of the ground, where it moves toward the warmer climates.

The unequal heating of Earth's surface causes another important wind pattern. If the air in a small area becomes heated more than the air around it, it expands and becomes lighter. This causes the pressure or weight of the air in that region to become less. Meteorologists call this a "low pressure area." If, on the other hand, air becomes cooler than the air around it, it's pressure increases. This is known as a "high pressure area." Air moves generally from a high toward a low.

But the air moving out of a high and into a low pressure area rarely moves in a straight line. The spinning of Earth below it causes the wind to curve. As the air leaves a high pressure area in the Northern Hemisphere, it begins to circle the area in a clockwise direction. And, as it nears the low pressure area it twists in a counterclockwise direction. South of the equator, these patterns are reversed.

A large, fairly stationary high pressure area called the Bermuda high has a great affect on hurricanes of the Atlantic Ocean, Caribbean Sea, and the Gulf of Mexico. This mass of heavy air has its center in the general area of the Bermuda Islands, near the center of the Atlantic. Near the surface of the ocean, the air moves in a generally clockwise direction out of this high. To the south of the high, these air currents are called the "easterlies" or the "easterly tradewinds." It was these winds that pushed the ships of Columbus from Spain to the West Indies.

Usually these winds flow smoothly around the Atlantic. At times, however, as the easterlies move over the warm waters of the tropical Atlantic Ocean, they break up into wisps of whirling air currents. Scientists think these wisps may start whirling around in tight circles because of the spinning of Earth about its axis. It is thought that this whirling current in the easterly flow of air may be the birth of a hurricane. Gathering heat and water vapor from the water below it, the air itself warms and expands, causing a low pressure area. The air around the low rushes in, twisting in a counterclockwise direction and gathering up more warm water vapor as it moves.

As the warm air rises, it becomes cooler. The water vapor changes into tiny water droplets. Clouds form, and rain begins to fall. As the water vapor condenses into liquid water, tremendous amounts of energy are released. Scientists think that it is this energy that may drive the intense winds of the full-blown hurricane.

But not all low pressure areas that develop inside the easterlies grow into hurricanes. Meteorologists have guessed that the movement of air at high altitudes may play a big part in this. They suggest that as the storm spins around itself, with warm, moist air feeding into it from below, the high-altitude wind system may carry the hurricane winds away from the top of the storm center. This would keep the low pressure area from "filling up" and dying out. If the winds spiral up around the center of the storm and then are quickly carried away, there would be room for more air to move in at the ocean's surface.

Scientists have taken all the information they have about all the hurricanes they have ever studied and put this information into a computer. The result is a description of an "average" hurricane. This average hurricane has an eye that is 14 miles across. On the average, the spiraling winds will move at speeds greater than 74 miles per hour over a circle that is 100 miles in diameter. There will be gale-force winds—above 40 miles per hour—over a 400-mile-diameter circle. The average life of a July storm is eight days. An August storm will go for 12 days, on the average.

But there is no such thing as an "average" storm. Each one is a unique individual. It would give us a better description of a hurricane if we were told that hurricanes happen as early as May or as late as November, but most of them occur in July, August, and September. Sometimes the eye is so small a plane can't safely turn around in it, but it is not unusual to find an eye 25 or 30 miles across its center.

Thus, we get a picture of winds blowing into a doughnut-shaped storm. This is a very flat doughnut that may be only ten miles high and 400 miles across. The winds spiral into the storm in bands. The radar picture will show a clear center surrounded by heavy clouds that trail fingers of lighter clouds in a curving pattern.

When a hurricane moves over land, it causes enormous amounts of destruction and loss of lives. Between 1960 and 1969, it is estimated that more than 432 million dollars worth of property was destroyed. Before our hurricane warning system was developed, thousands of lives were sometimes lost in a single year. Even now several hundred people can lose their lives in one storm alone.

Weather scientists are trying to find ways to cause

hurricanes to be less severe. *Stormfury* is a project in which scientists try to learn more about storms, and learn how to control them. They think that by seeding the storm clouds with millions of pellets of silver iodide they may be able to cause the storm to lose some of its fury. In order for rain to form, each droplet must have a speck of something as its center. That something may be a speck of dust or in this case silver iodide. Supplying centers for raindrops is called seeding the clouds. When clouds are seeded in this way they may give up their water vapor and thus also give up their energy.

Circular or cyclonic wind storms form over every ocean except the South Atlantic. It is thought that the waters there are too cold to feed such a storm. Although these storms are called by different names in different places of the world, they have the same cause, the same life pattern, and they result in much destruction for man wherever the two meet.

Another form of circular wind storm is the tornado. It usually blows in a counter clockwise direction and is found in most parts of the world. Those in the United States and Australia are said to be the most destructive. In the United States, tornadoes cause most of their damage in Texas, Oklahoma, Kansas, and Missouri, but they occur in any of the fifty states. Tornadoes usually are formed over land, but they have been known to happen over water. Then they are called waterspouts.

A tornado lasts a much shorter length of time than a hurricane, usually only minutes, or at the most a few hours. But its winds can be much stronger than a hurricane's and it destroys almost everything in its path. Tornadoes begin where two kinds of air masses meet.

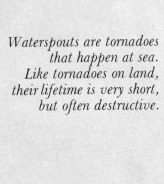

Waterspouts are tornadoes that happen at sea. Like tornadoes on land, their lifetime is very short, but often destructive.

When a warm, moist block of air meets a dry cold front, a tornado is possible. The hot air from a large forest fire has been known to trigger a tornado when it meets the colder air above. During World War II these storms were once born over Germany in the hot air that climbed from the city of Hamburg after it had been bombed.

It is not possible to say for sure when a tornado will form, but we do know what weather conditions to look for. When these weather conditions are just right, the Weather Service announces a tornado watch. This tells the people in a particular area that atmospheric conditions are just right for a tornado to form. When tornadoes are actually seen, either as echoes on a radar screen or first hand, by a person, a tornado warning is issued. People in a particular area will be told that a tornado has been sighted and they may be in its path. It is at this time that people who have received such a warning ought to find protection from the storm.

A tornado is seen as a whirling cylinder of air dipping out of the mass of overhead clouds. Sometimes more than one tornado will drop down from the same clouds. This slender rotating storm usually turns about a hollow area of very low pressure. This low air pressure causes an updraft that allows dirt, debris, houses, and people be picked up and moved from one place to another. Sometimes they are set down again gently, and sometimes they are smashed to the ground. Whole buildings, freight cars, and bridges have been moved. Straws and pieces of wood have been blown with such force that they have been imbedded in buildings, trees, and pieces of metal.

The low pressure of a tornado sometimes causes windows of buildings to burst outward when a tornado passes over. The air pressure inside the building does not drop as rapidly as the air outside. This causes the air in the building to press out on the windows with greater force than the air outside the building is pressing in. For the same reason, refrigerator doors sometimes pop open and people have trouble with their eardrums hurting. Sometimes, they find it hard to breathe.

Like a hurricane, the tornado has two kinds of motion: a rotating motion and a forward motion. The forward motion of the tornado has reached as much as 70 miles per hour. Usually tornadoes travel for very short distances—a few feet to a few miles. Then they are drawn back up into their parent cloud to disappear, or to dip down again minutes or hours later.

Man will probably never be able to control storms entirely, but understanding what causes them will help us to predict when and where a hurricane or a tornado may hit. These predictions will surely save many lives each year. If we can also learn how to make changes in these storms, so that their energy is released gradually instead of all at once, we can receive the rainfall we need without suffering the destruction.

VOLCANOES

THE CITY PEOPLE FORGOT

IT WAS THE SUMMER of the year 79 A.D. For many days there had been earth tremors, but this was not unusual in Pompeii. Gaius, who was twelve years old, was taking a message to his father. It was a hot August day and he had to walk all the way across town. His mind was more on the annoyance he felt at being given a job ordinarily done by a slave than it was on the frequent shaking of the ground beneath his feet.

His mother had insisted this message was too important for a slave to carry. Besides, the slaves were upset. A huge cloud seemed to be coming out of the tall mountain that stood above the Pompeian scenery. They felt it was a bad omen. The gods must be angry. The women wailed as they hovered inside their quarters.

The fear that gripped them seemed to be in the air. You could almost touch it. Gaius' younger sister held to her mother's skirts all morning. Even his mother, who usually ran her household calmly and efficiently was not herself today. She tried to hide her nervousness, but nevertheless she spoke sharply to Gaius when he complained about having to bear messages like a slave.

At least he would behave like a nobleman, he told himself. He was almost old enough to be considered a man, and he congratulated himself on the fact that he was not afraid. His father had reassured them just that morning that there was nothing to fear.

As Gaius walked through the forum, where the townspeople often gathered to hear politicians speak, he could see the mountain towering 10,000 feet above the marble columns outside the temples. It was about five miles away, but today it seemed much closer. The cloud was very strange looking, he thought. It looked like it came right out of the mountain top and went straight up—just like one of the marble pillars holding up the roof of the Temple of Apollo. Then, at a great height, it billowed out. It reminded him of the trunk and spreading branches of the trees that grew on the mountainside.

His eyes traveled from the cloud down the sides of the mountain. It was green everywhere, the mountain was covered with pine trees and shrubs. Here and there he could see the carefully tended vineyards. The grapes were ripe and sweet this time of year. He was comforted by the sight of those peaceful, luxurious fields and went on his way.

Pompeii was a busy, prosperous city in 79 A.D. As Gaius walked through the city he passed a bakery where grain was ground into flour and bread was made. The wonderful smell of fresh-baked bread reached him, and he inhaled deeply. It made him feel hungry even though he had just finished his mid-day meal. The many shops of the market area were closed during this hot part of the day. The craftsmen who made wool, glass, and items of silver and bronze were quiet. On the walls were painted slogans for the coming elections.

Many of the walls showed signs of damage done by an

earthquake that had shaken Pompeii seventeen years earlier. Of course, that was before Gaius was born, but he had heard his father's friends speak of it; there was even a temple to the gods on the forum square, built to show that the people were sorry for whatever wrongs they had committed to bring on such a terrible thing.

They had no way of knowing there was a connection between the now frequent movement of the earth beneath their feet and the cloud growing above the mountain on the horizon. There was no record of Mount Vesuvius having erupted in the past. But the people of Pompeii grew more and more anxious as they watched the cloud turn a dark color.

Gaius walked a little faster and tried not to think about the darkening cloud. Instead he turned his mind to the games that were to take place soon in the amphitheater. As soon as the crops were all in, there would be a big celebration. His thoughts were interrupted by the sight of his father coming out of the house where the thermal baths were. Wealthy Pompeians enjoyed these warm pools of water and often relaxed and talked with their friends while bathing there. His father was talking earnestly with some other men, and Gaius fell in step with them, knowing that he must not interrupt their conversation.

As they walked along, his father put his hand on the boy's shoulder. Gaius felt proud to be considered grown-up enough to be a part of their group. After a few minutes, Gaius' father asked what brought him out in the heat of the day, and Gaius guiltily remembered the message from his mother.

She wanted his father to come home as soon as he could. Gaius told his father the slaves were frightened by the newly formed cloud over the mountain. They were not able to do their work because they felt the gods were angry. They were afraid they were going to be punished for some unknown sins they had committed.

Gaius' father looked up at the cloud with a frown. It had now grown to such a size that it was between them and the sun. There seemed to be occasional bits of something in the air, something that looked like ashes. But there were no fires in Pompeii this time of day in the summer.

As they left the other men and started toward home, the sky became darker and a brisk wind brought larger pieces of ash and fine particles of dirt and sand into the air around them. Some of the bits of sand were really too large to be called sand. They were more like very tiny rocks. From the direction of the mountain, sounds that resembled rolls of thunder became louder and louder.

It seemed to Gaius a strange kind of storm, and he gripped his father's hand a little tighter. They reached their house by pushing their way through the small groups of people who now clogged the narrow walkways. Chariots being pulled through the streets were unable to get by the quickly gathering crowds.

Gaius noticed as they went in the door that his mother's usually calm, peaceful face was tense as she greeted them. He felt shocked when he realized she had been crying. There were sounds of wailing from the servants' quarters and his younger sister was sobbing in her mother's arms, while the other sister clung to her skirts.

The 1944 eruption of Mt. Vesuvius filled the southern Italian sky, a reminder of how the city of Pompeii was buried more than eighteen centuries earlier.

He listened to his father's calm voice and felt his sagging spirits rise as his father suggested they close the doors and windows to keep out the dust and dirt. His mother remembered the earthquake of 17 years before and suggested they stand out in the courtyard, where nothing could fall on them. But as they stepped out the door, they were caught in a rain of ashes and small stones. They couldn't stay out there. Besides, the air was heavy with a disagreeable smell that made it hard to breathe. Although it was still afternoon, it was almost dark outside.

As they closed the windows, they saw people moving through the streets toward the gates of the city. They were leaving the city, carrying packs of belongings. Some shielded their heads from the falling stones with pillows. Frantically they pushed past one another. They were leaving, but where could they go?

The servants entered the house in a group, and one of them stepped forward. He was a man older than Gaius' father and had been chosen as the spokesman. His hands trembled, and he could not control his voice as he implored the head of the house to take them out of the city, and far away from this terrible thing that was happening.

Gaius' father placed his hand on the old man's arm and spoke to him gently. He explained that there was nowhere to go outside the city walls. The closest city was Herculaneum, and it lay toward the mountain. In the other direction lay the sea. He felt they would be safer there, in the house. He said that fortune favored those who were brave. However, if the slaves wanted to leave, he would not stop them.

The slaves gathered together in a corner. After talking it over, all left except the old man, his wife, and grown daughter. They stayed inside with Gaius and his family while the rest quickly collected a few things and pushed their way through the streets toward the gates.

After most of their servants had fled Pompeii, Gaius' father gathered his family around him, including the old slave and his family. He spoke to them kindly and calmly. He reminded them that they had felt many earth shocks before, some of which were very destructive, but they had all survived them. He admitted that the falling dust, ashes, and stones were dangerous and the vapors in the air were disagreeable to smell, but he asked them to try to ignore these things. He suggested they have their dinner.

Gaius admired his father's courage and vowed to try to imitate it. He even played a game with his younger sisters—something he ordinarily would never do. His father sat down to read and his mother supervised the slaves in getting their evening meal ready.

The earth continued to shake. It seemed to Gaius, as he got ready for bed, that the shocks were stronger than ever. He wished they would quit. His father had said he would move the children's cots into their parents' room for the night. Although Gaius wouldn't admit it, even to himself, he felt better about going to bed in their room.

Outside, the ashes continued to fall, like snow. There was also a rain of tiny porous stones, lighter than most rocks. These pumice stones contained many air pockets and even though they were cooler than when hurled from the volcano, they were still too warm to touch. This cloud of ash and dust that covered Pompeii made it impossible to see even an outline of the huge mountain. Where they should have been able to see the top of the mountain, there was a red glow, like flames shooting up. Over the glow, the lightning snapped—more lightning than anyone had ever seen before in one place. It continued all night. The smell of sulfur was so strong in the city that it was more than just disagreeable. It was becoming difficult to breathe.

Gaius felt a hand on his shoulder and heard his father speak his name. He sat up suddenly, his heart beating faster. He heard the others moving about the room, but could hardly see them even though the lamp glowed softly on the table. The cloud outside seemed to have moved into the room with them. His father told him to get dressed. They would have to leave the city. His father gave no sign to the rest of the family of his fears that perhaps they were leaving too late.

The outside door was difficult to open because so much debris had piled against it. Once outside, they made their way through the crowds of people to the gate. Though it was dawn elsewhere in Italy, it was dark in Pompeii. People still pushed their way toward the gates, burdened with bundles of things they felt they couldn't leave behind. Like those who had left the evening before, some tied pillows on their heads to protect them from the falling stones. Others held pieces of tile or cloth over their heads. Everywhere was the sound of wailing and weeping. Mothers called their children. Old men called to their gods. Some feared it was the last eternal night on earth and there were no longer any gods to hear them.

Gaius and his family and slaves kept close together as they went through the streets. Once outside the gates, his father told them to get off the road so they wouldn't be trampled by the crowds. They were to walk through the fields, away from the lightning, which was all they could now see of Vesuvius. His father told them they must keep walking. They were not to sit down even if they were tired. The ashes were getting deep and walking was difficult. Breathing was also difficult and Gaius held one hand in front of his nose and mouth to keep out the ashes. He felt very sleepy. The darkness that was around him was not one of a moonless night. To him it was more like being in a room with no doors or windows.

The next day it began to get light, little by little. It was not like normal daylight, but rather like an eclipse of the sun. The air was full of mist and dust. The ground —indeed the entire city—was covered completely as if by a fresh, very deep snowfall. There were no trees to be seen—not even a building was in sight. All was completely covered. There was no movement anywhere. There was no sound.

As the mist rolled out to sea and the dust settled, Vesuvius looked over the place where the city had been. Vesuvius, which had two days ago been more than 10,000 feet tall, was now less than 4000 feet above sea level. The top 6000 feet of the mountain had been pulverized and blown across the countryside. Pompeii lay under 23 feet of ashes, dust and small stones. Three quarters of her people—approximately 15,000 people—lay buried with her.

Pompeii and her people were mourned by the entire country. A man known as Pliny the Younger wrote two letters describing what he had seen and felt from a nearby city. Martialis and Statius wrote sad poems about the disaster. Then everyone forgot Pompeii. Seeds blew in by the wind and were carried in by birds. Over the years, the ground covering Pompeii became a wilderness. No traces of the city were found, or even looked for, until about the year 1595 when Domenico Fontana made an underground aqueduct to carry water across that part of Italy. His aqueduct ran through a part of old Pompeii, but he was an engineer, not interested in archeology. The statues and vases he found did not lead to further searching.

Occasionally someone digging there found an object of interest and took it away, but it was almost like grave robbing. No scientific digging and restoring of the city was begun until 1748. Slowly, and with few interruptions, it has continued ever since.

Even today the work goes on. It is a job that must be done carefully to prevent the buildings and their contents from being damaged. The city covers an area of 161 acres—161 acres covered by more than 20 feet of volcanic ash that must be removed almost a spoonful at a time.

The rewards for this careful, time-consuming work are great, though. Today you can walk through the streets of the excavated parts of Pompeii. You can walk on the same paving stones the Pompeians walked on. You can examine the ruts that were worn in the stones by chariot wheels.

Walls of houses are still standing, complete with the pictures the Pompeians painted on them. The intricate designs of the mosaic floors are there to please anyone who looks. In the gardens are pools and fountains.

The walls along the streets are painted in red with the names and qualifications of men hoping to be elected to public office. Bread was found in the ovens at the bakery, wine in the wine cellars.

There is an outdoor theater and a smaller theater once used for music recitals. You can see the gladiators' barracks, the amphitheater for sports events, and the forum where political speeches were made.

The ash and dust, when rained upon, formed a somewhat hardened crust around the bodies of the people who died with Pompeii. The bodies have mostly disintegrated during all of these years, but the hardened ashes of Vesuvius have kept a record of their shape, even their clothes and sometimes the expressions on their faces. By a special process, the molds of some of these bodies have been filled with plaster and allowed to dry. When the mold is chipped away, there is a plaster statue that shows the outline of the person who was there. Even figures of animals have been re-formed in this way. Sometimes a group of figures is found together. One

Studying such ruins as these baths helps us to understand how people lived in 79 A.D. in Pompeii.

such group was found outside the walls of Pompeii. A boy and a younger girl lie side by side, as if asleep. A short distance away is a woman with a small child close to her. Behind all of them is a grown man, in a half-sitting position, as if he were trying to get up.

There have been other eruptions since Pompeii was buried in 79 A.D., but none so disasterous. For almost 1000 years after that date Vesuvius had minor upheavals, throwing out small amounts of solid fragments.

This is the usual way that an old, worn out volcano behaves. When it first begins, it sends out lava flows—molten rock that slithers out of the top or from cracks in the sides of the mountain.

As the lava hardens, it "tightens the lid" on the mountain. Not until great force is built up inside the mountain by the expanding gases does it blow off the top again. In the case of Vesuvius, this enormous explosion blew away the top two-thirds of the mountain. Later come smaller and smaller explosions until no more are heard. A volcano is said to be extinct when no more activity is observed for a long period of time.

Then, in the year 1036, a change took place in Vesuvius as new lava began to ooze from the mountain. It had entered a "second childhood." It was rejuvenated. Every few years a new lava flow was seen. In 1904 and again in 1905, lava came out of splits in the sides of the mountain. On April 4, 5, and 6, 1906, new lava mouths opened along the southern side of the mountain. Lava was first seen coming out of a place 500 feet below the top, then from another 1300 feet lower, and finally from another slit 600 feet lower still. These flows were not floods of lava, but were slow-moving. They were still destructive. Fields and houses were damaged. On April 7, a column of steam lifted dust particles four miles straight up from the crater. The cloud was laced with crackles of lightning. Ashes fell on the nearby village of Boscotricano, collapsing roofs. For two weeks the explosions inside the mountain could be heard. Gradually the mountain became quiet.

It has been heard from occasionally since then, but no real damage has been done. In 1944, when the battles of World War II were dotted over Europe, Vesuvius again exploded, and poured out more lava, dust and ash. The Germans and Americans had just been fighting in that area and the battle line was now only 70 miles away. At Naples, an American photographer took pictures of the cloud over Vesuvius.

There was only one man left to attend to the observatory on the side of Mount Vesuvius. Imagine his disappointment that the misfortunes of war had made it impossible to get film for his cameras. The only close-hand records were from the observatory's scientific instruments and his own written words.

The observatory still records seventy to eighty shocks a day from Vesuvius. Most of them are too small to be felt by a person. But if you go up to the top of the mountain and down a little way into the crater, you can place your hand on the sides of the crater and feel its warmth. If you blow your breath against the warm rocks there, the moisture from your breath will cause a small puff of steam to rise. And in the imaginative mind, there will be no doubt that Vulcan, the Greek god of fire, lies sleeping beneath Vesuvius.

THE VALLEY OF TEN THOUSAND SMOKES

CAPTAIN K. W. PERRY, skipper of the U.S. steamer *Manning*, stood on his deck watching the dock crews load coal aboard. The time was four o'clock in the afternoon of June 6, 1912. The port was St. Paul, a small village on the Alaskan island of Kodiak. Glancing idly across the island toward the west he noticed a peculiar cloud that seemed to be rapidly growing from the horizon. "A snow cloud," he thought. "Late in the year for snow, I should think." Making a mental note to watch the progress of the storm, he wrote the time in his log.

An hour later the cloud covered about one-fourth of the western sky and a light snow began to fall. Captain Perry stepped back onto the deck, so as to see the cloud better. Suddenly, he realized that it was not snow that was drifting ahead of the gray mass above him, but tiny, floating bits of ash!

By six o'clock the face of the cloud had passed over the ship and the fall of ash had increased. Perry called to his ship's officers, ordering them to get the entire crew on deck and to begin cleaning the fine layer of dust from the ship. "We have only three hours until sunset," he told them. "I want the ship clean by then."

But Captain Perry was wrong about the amount of time his crew had to clean the ship. Within an hour— a full two hours before sunset, darkness fell. "A black night," Perry described that afternoon in his log. Throughout the long night ash continued to fall, while lightning flashed and thunder rolled through the blackness. At nine the next morning, a dim sun shone weakly through the reddish haze. Five inches of ash covered everything in sight—houses, wharves, ships. Streams and wells were choked with the white, snow-like stuff, and the *Manning* began to supply fresh water to the citizens of St. Paul.

By noon the *Manning's* crew had no sooner finished clearing the ship of the heavy ash than it began again. This time the darkness came even earlier, around two in the afternoon. The smell of sulfur choked the sailors as they used their brooms, shovels, and fire hoses to clear the decks, this time by lantern light. The sound of avalanches of ash could be heard dully as the accumulated weight on the sides of the hills became too great and tons of debris poured down the slopes. Strange-shaped lightning flashes cut through the darkness and the men talked of the stories they had heard of Pompeii.

By the afternoon of June 8, the fall of ash slowed somewhat and the people of St. Paul could dimly see again. Occasionally, the ground would shake beneath their feet, and their lungs choked with dust and ash, but it was apparent the worst was over.

It was clear to every educated person in the area that a volcano had erupted with a tremendous explosion. On June 6, its sound was heard in the city of Juneau, almost 750 miles due east, and its dust had settled to the earth

900 miles away, in Ketchikan. Near Iliamma Bay, over 100 miles away, it was reported later "the earth never ceased to move for twelve hours." But no one knew where the active volcano was.

Several days later, when the mail steamer *Dora* arrived at Seward, the first real information was flashed to the world. On the sixth, the *Dora* had been cruising in the Shelikof Straits that separate Kodiak Island from the Alaskan Peninsula. At about three in the afternoon, the *Dora's* crew heard a tremendous explosion and saw a heavy column of what appeared to be smoke rise over the mainland. The skipper of the steamer took a bearing on the smoke and decided that it came from the 7500-foot-tall Mount Katmai that stood some 55 miles away.

By six that evening, the *Dora* was groping her way through a heavy, unnatural blackness. "We could not even see the water passing the side of the ship!" the captain reported later.

At first, it seemed the little ship might make the safety of one of the many harbors of Kodiak Island, but darkness closed in on them before they could find a safe channel. Setting a course for the safer open sea, the *Dora* felt its way up the coast through the darkness, which lasted for 24 hours. "Even the birds couldn't fly through the clouds," the crew reported later. "Dozens of them fell to the deck all through that long night."

Geologists in the United States were surprised at the *Dora's* report that Mount Katmai had erupted. The ancient mountain was a volcano, all right. There was no doubt of that. But it had lain quietly for so many generations that even the local Indians had no legends about it. Any one of a hundred other Alaskan volcanoes might

be expected to erupt at any time, since dozens of them constantly produced steam. Minor, local earthquakes were an everyday occurrence in the huge territory. But it was difficult to believe that the *Dora's* captain had not made a mistake in his sightings. However, after a search of several weeks, some eye-witnesses were found, and their stories seemed to show that the report from the *Dora* was correct.

Near the coast, almost 20 miles south of Mount Katmai, was the little Indian village of Katmai. During the summer, the village's entire population moved farther down the coast to the fishing village of Cold Bay, where they could find work. In the year 1912, this movement of the village people had taken place on June 4, just two days before the explosion. For some unexplained reason, two families had stayed behind this year, and thus became the nearest human beings to survive the eruptions.

It was not until after the explosions began and the air was filled with flying ash and rocks that these families finally fled their village. In their tiny skin boats, they paddled furiously south along the coast and away from the thundering giant behind them. They arrived safely at Cold Bay, their boats badly damaged by flying peb-

Mt. Katmai, Alaska. To the right is the flat expanse of land known as the "Valley of the 10,000 Smokes."

Mt. Shishaldin, an active volcano in Alaska. Even its glacier exterior cannot hide the warning of the smoking peak.

bles, and gasped out their story to their friends. "The top of Katmai hill burn off!" they said.

It wasn't until six years later that another eyewitness was found. An old man called "American Pete" was dying of tuberculosis when he was found by the leader of an American scientific party. Yes, he had been near the mountain that day, nearly as close as the Katmai villagers but on the other side, toward the north.

American Pete was the chief of a tribe of Indians who lived in a village called Savonoski, on the shores of Lake Naknek. The Savonoski Indians took fish from the lake and its streams. They hunted caribou, moose, and bear in a heavily wooded valley that ran toward the north from the base of Mount Katmai. At the opposite end of the valley from the mountain, they had built a cluster of huts to stay in overnight when they were hunting in the valley. American Pete had gone alone to the hunting camp on the afternoon of June 6.

"The Katmai Mountain blow up with lots of fire, and fire come down trail from Katmai with lots of smoke," he told the American scientist. "Me go fast Savonoski. Everybody get in skin boats. Dark. No could see. Hot ash fall."

No one will ever know whether there were other witnesses to the explosions of June 6, 1912, and it is likely that if there were, they did not survive. It is fortunate for American Pete that he "go fast Savonoski," for the valley that he was in changed suddenly that day, and every living thing in it died.

The rest of the world knew nothing about the changes in American Pete's valley until almost four years after the eruptions.

The discovery of what happened in the valley was made by a team of scientists sent by the National Geographic Society in 1916. They were to climb and survey what was left of Mount Katmai. They found the top of the mountain had, indeed, disappeared—almost 1000 feet of it. In its place was a huge caldera that measured $3\frac{1}{2}$ by $2\frac{1}{2}$ miles, and almost a half mile deep. In the bottom of the caldera was a sparkling blue lake, with a tiny island that had been pushed up in its center. It was when the scientists began their survey of the northern slopes of the mountain that they first saw what was left of American Pete's valley.

Here was a long, narrow valley, not gently rolling and tree covered as they had expected, but almost perfectly flat. The director of the team described what he first saw like this: "Great columns of white vapor poured out of the fissured ground, rising gracefully until they mingled in a common cloud which hung between the walls of the valley. The whole valley as far as the eye could reach, was full of hundreds, no thousands—literally tens of thousands of smokes curling up from its floor." And, in this way, the "Valley of Ten Thousand Smokes" was discovered and named.

Another discovery was made by this group of scientists. To the west of Mount Katmai about five miles, they discovered a new, active volcano, which they named "Novarupta." This discovery may be even more important to the solution of the mystery of what happened in June of 1912 than the discovery of the Valley of Ten Thousand Smokes.

It was not until two summers later that a group of scientists could explore the valley carefully. Their most surprising discovery was that the flat floor of the valley was not caused by an ordinary flow of lava, as they had expected. Instead, they found the valley to be covered with a fine-grained sand that had apparently washed through the valley at the time of the eruptions.

It is now thought, by some scientists at least, that this sand was very, very hot at the time it flowed from the mountain. Probably, since it acted very much like a flowing liquid, it was mixed with a great amount of gas from the magma below the surface. As the super-hot gas rushed up through cracks in the earth, it must have picked up rocks and broken them into sand-sized particles. When this mixture of sand and gas reached the surface of the earth, it flowed down the valley, like Pelée's "glowing cloud." The major difference between this "cloud" and that of Mount Pelée would seem to be that the one that flowed through the Valley of Ten Thousand Smokes was very much heavier. Therefore, it hugged the ground, killing only those living things it actually touched.

And kill it did, but apparently no human beings were trapped by this "glowing cloud." When the scientists arrived in the valley they found the hot sand had burned all of the life from an area of 53 square miles. It buried the valley for a length of over 20 miles, and a width of about 9 miles at the widest point. At first, no one could guess how deep the sand lay in the valley. More recent studies show that, in places, the sand is 700 feet deep! The total weight of sand that flowed out into the valley must have been nearly 30 million tons!

After the sand had cooled and the gas had escaped, the floor of the valley began to explode. Evidence of this is seen in the hundreds of small volcanic craters that pock-mark the otherwise smooth sand. And then, through these craters or through fissures opened by the pressure below, steam began to escape. The scientists measured the temperature of the escaping gas. In many of the vents it was well over 500° F, and one had a temperature of nearly 1200° F. To give you some idea of how hot this hotter temperature is, it is nearly the melting point of aluminum, and well above the melting points of both lead and zinc!

The destruction of living things was so complete in the valley that the team of scientists found it necessary to bring in everything they would need in packs on their backs. This included not only their food, clothing and tents, but also all the wood they would need. Naturally, they did not want to pack in wood for their cooking fires, if they could help it. They soon discovered they could swing a cooking pot from a rope and lower it into one of the steam vents. After cooking a few meals this way, however, they found that the steam contained some type of acid. This acid ate into the ropes so that they were weakened and broke easily. Eventually, the acid steam even ate holes in the bottom of the iron pots!

Since 1916, many groups of scientists have studied the area around the Valley of Ten Thousand Smokes. This is now called Katmai National Monument, named for the large volcano in its center. As a result of all this study, there has been a new theory suggested, that perhaps explains what happened in 1912 a little more completely than did the stories of the Indian eye-witnesses. This new idea suggests that Mount Katmai was *not* the mountain that exploded. Instead, many scientists now think it was the new volcano, Novarupta, that erupted and threw so much ash and rock over the Alaskan Peninsula and Kodiak Island. It seems almost certain that it was Novarupta, or at least the magma below it, that produced the heavy "glowing cloud" that covered the valley.

But, if this idea is true, what happened to the top of Mount Katmai?

This newest theory on the collapse of Mount Katmai suggests that the vent of Novarupta opened into the same magma pocket that lies under Mount Katmai (and under the Valley of Ten Thousand Smokes). When Novarupta exploded so violently, the pressure on the magma must have been released. This must have allowed the whole magma to shift somewhat, leaving a hollow space below Mount Katmai, five miles away. Thus, the whole top of the mountain simply fell into the empty space left by the moving magma.

Will the thousands of steaming vents release enough of the pressure on the magma below Novarupta and the valley to keep it from erupting again? Scientists think this is probably what is happening since many of the vents have slowed or stopped their release of steam. But the chain of islands and the Alaskan Peninsula contain about 80 volcanoes, more than half of which are considered to be active. It seems probable that we will hear more about the volcanoes in this area in the future.

WINDOWS INTO THE EARTH

WHAT DO YOU THINK of when the word "volcano" is mentioned? Most people think of a huge mountain, perhaps with a column of smoke coming from its top. But not all volcanoes form mountains. Some volcanic eruptions come from fairly flat ground. The important part of a volcano is the opening or vent from the surface of the earth to a melted mass or rock which is generally no deeper than 40 miles. This vent is the "window" through which scientists have learned so much about the center of our planet.

Scientists have learned a great deal more about the sun and the moon than they have about the center of the earth. The deepest oil wells reach only about five miles into the earth. These are but pin-pricks in the surface of our planet, which is almost 8000 miles in diameter. You can easily understand why scientists are excited when a volcano begins to throw out materials from 40 miles below.

The drilling of oil wells and the digging of mines have revealed that the temperature of the earth increases the deeper we go. No one really knows why this happens. The amount of this increase in temperature varies at different places on the earth, but it averages about one Fahrenheit degree for every 60 feet of depth. In other words, at one mile below the surface, we would expect the temperature to be about 150° F, and at ten miles the temperature might be well over 1000° F! And, at depths below 20 miles, it is probably well above the melting point of most rocks.

Scientists have been able to perform several types of experiments which seem to show that rocks at the center of the earth are *not* liquid, in spite of the high temperature that must exist there. They think this is true because of the very high pressure at the center of the earth, caused by the weight of the rocks above. When a crack appears in the surface crust of the earth, this pressure is reduced and the rocks far below the surface at that point may become soft enough to flow.

In some way that scientists do not yet understand, the heat from the center of the earth melts some of the rock nearer the surface of the earth—say some 30 or 40 miles down. This mass is apparently made not only of melted rock, but also of many kinds of gases that are dissolved in the melted rock. The whole thing—the liquid rock and the gases in it—is called magma as long as it is under the ground.

Since the magma is fairly near the surface of the earth, it begins to cool a little. As it does, the gases in it, which are mostly steam, separate from the rock and begin to build up tremendous pressures. Because of these pressures, the magma begins to move—sometimes sideways but more often upward, following weak places in the rocks. As it nears the surface of the earth, the weight of the rocks above and the temperature of the magma both become less. As a result, more and more gas escapes, and the pressure inside the magma becomes very

Cinder cones such as this in the Canadian Kastline Plateau are formed when tephra (ash, cinders and pumice) is thrown from a volcano as it erupts.

great. You have seen the force of gas escaping from a liquid when you open a bottle of soda pop. Before you remove the cap, the gases are dissolved in the liquid, but once the pressure is removed, out they come!

Usually, by the time the magma reaches the surface, it has lost most of the gases that were dissolved in it. From this point on, the scientists refer to it as lava. Lavas are of two general types. Some, such as those produced by Parícutin, are quite thick, like toothpaste. These pasty lavas are usually light in color. Since they do not flow easily, they form very rough, broken, jagged flows. The other type of lava will often produce flat fields with smooth or only slightly wrinkled surfaces, since it is very thin and flows readily.

TYPES OF VOLCANOES

The *Pelean* type of volcano, named after Mount Pelée, can be the most dangerous, since it often explodes without warning. In this type of volcano the magma is so thick it cannot flow at all. As the steam and other gases escape and the pressure builds higher and higher, the almost-solid magma is pushed upward through the vent. Because of this, the vent becomes almost completely clogged and the gases cannot escape.

Finally the pressure becomes so great that a violent explosion takes place, usually tearing a hold in the side of the cone. The glowing cloud that is usually formed by the Pelean type of volcano is made up of the hot gases that were at one time dissolved in the magma. As in the case of Mount Pelée, the cloud is often heavier than air and follows the slope of the cone downward, killing everything on the ground. Occasionally, the glowing cloud will be light enough to rise upward into the air, and very little damage will be done.

The *Vesuvian* type of eruption was named for Mount Vesuvius. Krakatoa is another example of this type of volcano, even though it is under water.

The first sign that a Vesuvian volcano has "come alive" again is the release of a tremendous amount of gas. This shows that the magma is moving, cooling down, and releasing gases. Often a small cone will be built up around the mouth of the vent, made of the ash and cinders that have been brought up by the escaping steam.

This is followed by a flow of rather thick lava, which cools almost immediately and clogs the mouth of the vent. For several days, or perhaps several months, the volcano will lie quietly. But beneath the surface more gases are escaping from the magma. They cannot escape through the vent and into the open air because of the now-solid lava that blocks the opening. Finally, a tremendous explosion occurs, throwing huge amounts of ash, cinders, blocks, and bombs into the air. Once the pressure is released, the Vesuvian volcano goes into a long resting stage, and slowly begins to build up strength for its next explosion.

A third type of volcano is named for the 3000-foot-high mountain, Stromboli. This volcano forms a tiny island in the Mediterranean Sea off the coast of Sicily, and has been in almost constant eruption for the last 2500 years! Because of this, Stromboli has been called "The Lighthouse of the Mediterranean."

Violent explosions from *Strombolian* type volcanoes are rare. This is because the magma is very, very fluid and hot enough so it never becomes completely solid. The escaping steam causes many small, frequent explosions that rarely do more than throw the glowing lava into the air. The steam cloud hangs over the top of the mountain almost constantly and reflects the glow from the lava that fills the crater below it. At night, this glow can be seen for miles in all directions, warning ships of the presence of the island. This is how Stromboli got its nickname.

Mauna Lao and Kilauea, in Hawaii, produce lava that is even less thick than that of the Strombolian type volcanoes. *Hawaiian* type volcanoes rarely explode violently. Instead, they produce large flows of thin, rope-like lava that spread out to form a large shield.

The last type of volcano is named the *Icelandic* type, although much of the volcanic activity of the northwestern United States was also of this type. We have very few good descriptions of this type of flow, since the last one occurred in Iceland in 1783. Even so, scientists have still succeeded in discovering many things about Icelandic volcanoes.

The lava from this type of volcano is very thin, much like that from the Hawaiian type. The major differences between these two types are the type of vents from which the lava flows, and the amounts of lava produced. In the Icelandic type of volcano, many huge fissures are produced, rather than a single (or at most, a few) small vent. From these large cracks in the ground, tremendous amounts of lava pour out. This thin lava flows out evenly over the land around the fissures, filling the valleys and covering the hills. When it cools, the lava forms a large area of flat land called a plateau that may be tens of thousands of square miles in size.

TYPES OF CONES

As you might expect, volcanoes produce different types of mountains, depending upon what happens to the cone as it is being formed. If, like Parícutin, the volcano produces mostly tephra, a cinder cone may be produced. Since these mountains are made almost entirely of material that fell to the ground in solid form, their sides are often quite steep—sometimes as steep as 40 degrees with the horizon. How steep they are depends mostly upon the size of the particles that formed the cone. You can experiment with this by letting sand fall slowly through your fingers from about a foot or so off the ground. You will discover that the shape of each "cone" you build will be almost the same, regardless of its size. "Cinder cones" are formed in much the same way but using larger particles (such as gravel) or smaller particles (such as flour) will give you mountains with different shapes.

The islands of Hawaii are formed in another way. Here the volcano vents produced very little tephra. Instead, the islands were formed almost entirely from lava flows. Since the lava was fairly fluid, the mountains have gently sloping sides, and are almost always much wider at the base than they are high. These are called *shield volcanoes.*

Most of the volcanic mountains in the world seem to be a mixture of both cinder cones and shield volcanoes. Scientists call these types *composite cones.* Sometimes they are called *strato-volcanoes,* since they are made of alternating layers of cinders and lava flows.

Most of the world's largest volcanoes are of the composite type. You have probably heard of Mount Fujiyama in Japan or Africa's Kilimanjaro. The slopes of the sides of mountains of this type are not as steep as those of cinder cones, or as gentle as those of shield volcanoes.

WHAT GOOD ARE VOLCANOES?

You have read about the destructive power of volcanoes. They have buried dozens of villages and cities beneath tons of lava or ash. They have killed a large number of people and a much larger number of animals and plants. But think for a minute about the *good* that can result because of volcanoes.

Farmers who live on the sides of volcanoes do so because their crops grow well there. The ash that is spread over the countryside by an active volcano is usually quite rich in certain minerals that plants need in order to grow. So, as soon as the ground has cooled enough, many brave people will move back to raise crops in order to take advantage of the fertile soil produced by the mountain.

The clouds of ash rising from Taal, in the Philippines, warn nearby residents that this volcano still lives!

IT
CAN
HAPPEN
AGAIN

THIS IS A BOOK about great catastrophes of the past — the fire that destroyed Chicago in 1871, the flood that swept through a valley in West Virginia in 1972, the great San Francisco earthquake in 1906. We read these stories and think, "I'm glad *I* wasn't there when that happened."

But are these really catastrophes of the past? Can they happen again? A glance at the daily newspaper shows that disaster can strike almost anyplace in the world and at almost any time.

Disaster struck in the middle of April, 1979, in Wichita Falls, Texas. Families watched TV while they prepared supper, because the weather had been threatening all afternoon. It was a few minutes after six in the evening.

White letters began to run quickly across the television screen. They moved so fast the youngsters could not read all of them. Suddenly, the sound of the show faded out and a loud BEEEEP took its place.

The announcer's voice was calm as he announced that a *tornado watch* was in effect. A funnel had touched the ground near the city. Everyone was advised to take cover.

One family hurried to their car. Perhaps the shopping center had a basement storm shelter. The sky was very, very dark as they drove through the nearly-deserted streets. Gusts of wind rocked the car and blew paper along the street in front of it. Bits of sand and gravel stung their faces and arms as they hurried across the parking lot and into the shopping mall.

They found no basement storm shelter. Hundreds of people lay on the cement floors of the shops, as far away from the glass doors and windows as possible. Outside, the sky grew even darker.

The wind had now grown so strong it carried pieces of lumber torn from the houses it had destroyed. Even pieces of bricks and metal flew through the air. The junk swirled around in a huge circle, rather than blowing in a straight line. Cars rolled down the streets and across the parking lots like a bunch of marbles.

The funnel struck directly at the shopping center. The cement and steel walls held, but the glass doors and windows did not. Pieces of glass swept through the air like swords. Merchandise from the shops was picked up and smashed against walls and people. Many people were badly hurt by the flying objects, but no one in the shopping center was killed.

Others were not so lucky. Before the day was over, the tornado system claimed at least 58 lives along the banks of the Red River. At least four tornadoes swept along the 50 miles between Vernon, Texas and Lawton, Oklahoma, but Wichita Falls was the hardest hit. Here three funnels seemed to join together, forming one huge funnel a quarter of a mile wide. Its winds reached an estimated 225 miles per hour — strong enough to lift cars and semi-trailers into the tops of trees, pull houses apart as if they were made of paper, and throw smaller debris a mile into the sky. A ten-mile long path of destruction was cut through the city.

This disaster struck at the people of the Red River

An example of the damage caused by a disastrous tornado in Witchita Fall, Texas, in April 1979.

Valley without warning and without mercy. They buried their dead, cleaned up the debris, and began rebuilding their city and their lives. But they always watch the sky for warnings of the next catastrophe.

It was also the middle of April, 1979 when another disaster struck half way around the world in Yugoslavia. Early in the morning of April 15, the rocks deep beneath the ocean floor slipped. Shock waves from the earthquake sped through the earth in all directions. As they reached the shoreline, they caused highways to slump into the sea. Buildings swayed, shuddered, and collapsed. Houses crumpled, crushing the people sleeping inside.

Eight and a half hours later, the earth began shaking again. Buildings that had been weakened by the first shock collapsed. But, except for the people still trapped in the debris and the rescue crews, there were no people around to be injured.

About 100 people were killed by this earthquake, and more than 1,200 were injured. This terrible disaster had followed an even worse earthquake by less than seven months.

In September, 1978, 25,000 people died in a minute and a half. This was in Iran, a country where the people are used to earthquakes. Scientists have recorded more than 20,000 earthquake shocks in the country in the last 18 years!

There were 100 small villages scattered on the edge of the deserts near the oasis named Tabas. The evening breezes had begun and most of the people were at home. They were enjoying their evening meals or were sitting outside, relaxing after a day of hard work in the terrible desert heat. Ninety seconds later, the entire region was a pile of dirt and twisted metal. Of the 17,000 people who had lived in Tabas, only 2,000 remained alive. The story was much the same in the smaller surrounding villages.

As terrible as this earthquake was, the worst perhaps the world has ever seen was in China on July 28, 1976. This disaster hit the city of Tangshan without warning at about 3:30 in the morning. The citizens of Tangshan were all asleep and were trapped in their beds.

The Communist government of China has not released complete details on this catastrophe, but we know that this was an industrial area, crowded with factories and workers. We also know that an area of the city nearly 20 square miles in size was leveled by the earthquake. Our scientists estimate that perhaps as many as 750,000 people died during the quake.

Eruption of the Kilauea Volcano, Hawaii, in September 1977.

For the past few years, the world has been spared from the terrible destruction that can be caused by an erupting volcano. But for two months during the summer of 1977, volcanoes in three widely separated parts of the world threatened their human neighbors with death and destruction.

In early August, Mount Usu in Japan erupted. Rocks and ash spewed from the 2,385-foot-high mountain. Millions of dollars worth of crops were destroyed, and 10,000 people were forced to leave their homes to avoid being killed. When they returned, they found their homes and belongings buried under a foot of ash and rock.

Later in the same month, Italy's famous Mount Etna began to rumble. This huge volcano towers nearly two miles above sea level and has erupted 140 times in the recorded history of the people who make their homes at its base.

The world's most active volcano is in Hawaii. Its name is Kilauea. During the month of September, 1977, the scientists who watch the monster carefully reported, "She's going full blast!" The people in the city of Hilo watched carefully as the lava spilled out of the vents in the side of the mountain. Living only

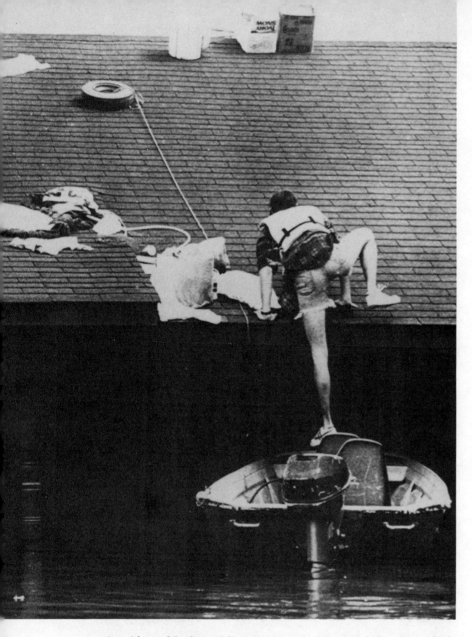

A resident of Jackson, Mississippi, retrieving some belongings which he had placed on the roof out of reach of the flood waters.

24 miles away from an active volcano, they have learned to expect disaster to strike at any moment.

Floods are another disaster that can strike almost anywhere at anytime, as the people who live in Central Mississippi found out during April in 1979. This flood was not caused by a bursting dam but simply by too much rain. Ten to 20 inches fell in a 24-hour period. The next day, the Pearl River pushed its way over the levees and into the city of Jackson.

By noon the next day the river was 20 feet over flood level. The silt-filled, yellow water was washing through many homes. Businesses were closed and streets were impassable in many parts of the city.

Four days later the river crested at 25 feet above flood stage. More than 80,000 homes were flooded, some with only their roof tops showing above the swirling water. Early warning of the coming flood saved the lives of many people, but their belongings were gone forever.

Other floods in the spring of 1979 did millions of dollars worth of damage in Houston and Beaumont, Texas, and farmers in Minnesota and North Dakota watched helplessly as their crops drowned when the Red River of the north overflowed.

April, 1979, was also a month of fire disasters. Eight elderly people died in Pennsylvania in a fire that swept their home on April 1. The cause was an overloaded electrical fuse box.

The next day, 25 people were killed in a retirement home in Missouri when a fire destroyed the entire building. An electrical short circuit caused this disaster.

A few days earlier, in late March, fire swept through two hotels in Boston. Smoke spread through the buildings quickly and 69 people had to be taken to hospitals. Several of these later died. It was discovered that a total of 13 blazes had been set by an arsonist in the two hotels.

Less than a year earlier, one of the strangest, most unusual fire and explosion disasters of history occured. It happened in Spain, in a campground on the coast of the Mediterranean Ocean. Hundreds of families had come from as far away as France to enjoy their summer vacation camping.

It was around noon on July 11, 1978. Most of the campers had returned from the beach and were gathered around their tents. The sun was shining. The weather was warm. Everyone was having a good time. Disaster was the farthest thing from their minds.

There didn't appear to be anything different about the truck, either. It was an ordinary tank truck, the kind we see on the highway quite often. This one was carrying a load of propylene gas, put into the truck under pressure so that it would be a liquid. The truck was heading for a factory farther down the coast where the gas was to be used for fuel. The driver of the truck knew there was some danger in carrying an explosive gas, but he had driven the truck for years and disaster was not something he thought about very often.

No one will ever know exactly what happened. The truck suddenly began to weave. Then it went into a skid. The driver fought the wheel, but the heavy truck was out of control. As it reached a spot above the campground, it turned over, rolled across the highway, and smashed through a cement wall. Below the wall was the campground and the campers.

The gas exploded as the tank truck hit the ground. This set off hundreds of other explosions throughout the camp as the heat reached gasoline in cars and the fuel the campers used in their cooking stoves.

More than 200 people were killed immediately by the explosions. At least 50 more were seriously burned and many of these died later. The total death count will never be known, because many of the bodies were thrown 150 yards into the sea.

Those of us who live in Canada and the northern parts of the United States know snowstorms will cause us some problems each winter. Transportation is disrupted. Schools and businesses close. Electric power is lost. We expect these things each year and take steps to prevent them from becoming a disaster.

But no one expects snowstorms to act like hurricanes. This is exactly how the blizzards of 1978 did act — like hurricanes with winds of 100 miles an hour and tides pushing over the beaches, plus tons and tons of snow and sub-zero temperatures.

A near-record snowfall blanketed New York on January 20, 1978, with 13.6 inches in one day. As the final traces of this storm were finally removed, another formed over North Carolina. Following the usual path of such storms, it moved off the coast and into the Atlantic Ocean. As it gathered moisture from the ocean, it moved northward toward New England.

On February 5, snow began to fall again. This was a Sunday, so the storm was more fun than trouble. But it continued all day Monday, and by midnight, 16.5 inches had fallen on New York City and the surrounding countryside. Winds gusted to nearly 50 miles per hour, closing roads for long periods of time. Thousands of people had to abandon their cars on the snow-choked highways and find shelter in firehouses, schools, churches, and even one factory.

In New Jersey, the high winds pushed tides to seven feet above normal. Severe flooding and erosion of beaches were reported along the coast.

North of New York City, in Massachusetts, the wind reached 92 miles an hour. (Winds above 74 miles an hour are considered to be "hurricane force.") A 700-foot-long oil tanker, with a crew of 33 people, radioed that it was taking on water and asked for help from the Coast Guard.

The Weather Service predicted that the storm would stop by dawn on Tuesday. However, one of the private weather predicting services told the New York City Sanitation Department to expect at least 25 inches of snow. Because of this prediction, the City kept its snow-removal crews at work.

Sure enough, the storm continued into Tuesday, February 7. The Sanitation Department had to plow the streets again and again as the snow continued to fall and gusts of wind of nearly 40 miles per hour blew it back into the cleared streets. Schools and most businesses were closed for the second day, with plans not to reopen anytime soon.

Meanwhile, the high tides continued to flood the coastlines of New Jersey. National Guard trucks and Coast Guard amphibious vehicles were used to evacute hundreds of people from their seaside homes. Inland, they found tons of snow piled into ten-foot-high drifts in some places.

In New England, the winds became so strong that windows were smashed. More than two feet of snow fell and was pushed into hugh drifts by the nearly 100-mile an hour winds. The states of Connecticut, Massachusetts, and Rhode Island were declared "disaster areas" by President Carter.

Reports of deaths began to come into the police and hospitals. Heart attacks were suffered while people tried to dig their stalled cars from drifts. People were killed by carbon monoxide poisoning sitting in cars stuck in the snow and running their engines to keep the heaters going. Some people died of exposure to the cold (the chill factor reached 50° below zero in the strong wind!). And some people died of drowning on the flooded beaches. Before the storm finally ended and the mess was cleaned up, a total of 99 lives were lost!

So, disasters are not something that happened to people in the past. They are a part of our everyday lives. By reading about them, we can learn how to prevent some of them and how to protect ourselves from others.

Index